ALPHA
IS THE NEW
BETA

PRAISE FOR *ALPHA IS THE NEW BETA*

"Dr. Martin is a powerful voice and leader for our affordable housing industry. He understands it's all about the residents and their dreams of future success."

—**Leticia Van de Putte,**
Former State Senator and Texas House Representative

"I know Dr. Cyrus Martin very well. I have actual experience with him in a counselor setting and with him in a business environment. As he found, I agree that minds improve, expand, and strengthen as a result of practiced mindfulness and that alpha executives with top-down requirements who actively use a mindful approach, benefit themselves and their colleagues. The audience for this book will find unlimited enlightenment with the guidance presented here."

—**Jot Couch**
Founder, Oaklake

"Where discussions on current social norms often force individuals into an 'alpha' versus 'beta' mindset, Dr. Martin's new work brilliantly cuts through this inaccurate dichotomy to establish a more nuanced understanding. His thorough analysis translates into concrete steps for professional and personal development, enabling a shift towards the Sigma mindset. This book is highly recommended not only for clinical professionals but also for those seeking to drive substantial growth in the business sector."

—**Craig Cristler**
CEO, Support Ninja

"Dr. Martin's innovative 'Sigma Mindset' will transform your experience of self and others. The combination of his research and experience validate the importance of self-awareness, flexibility, and authenticity in challenging the outdated framework of what it means to be 'alpha' and the archaic notion of success. This book fosters insight into what our emotions are communicating and creates a blueprint to elevate personal and professional relationships."

—Staci Passe, Ph.D.
Founder, Be Someone Therapy

Dr. Martin's research on mindfulness in counselors-in-training offers a compelling look into how regular mindfulness practices positively impact both emotional well-being and professional effectiveness. The findings reveal that mindfulness not only enhances the counselors' ability to manage stress and maintain balance but also provides tangible changes to the brain that foster resilience, focus, and compassion. Through these insightful discoveries, Dr. Martin highlights the profound role mindfulness can play in improving the personal and professional lives of helping professionals.

—Paul Caluscos
Co-Founder, The Well Nest

"Forget alpha vs. beta – Dr. Cyrus Martin introduces the Sigma Mindset: a transformative blend of mindfulness, authenticity and purpose that creates a real-world approach to leadership, allowing you to be true to yourself while supporting growth of others and making a real impact. A real need in today's business world!"

—Jessica Ghram
CFO, Tuscon Division Banner Health

"This is a powerful, unflinching work by one of the most thoughtful minds I've had the privilege to learn from. It challenges you to look inward, sit with discomfort, and grow through it. The insights are as emotionally raw as they are necessary—this book will stay with you long after the last page."

—Ben Irwin, LCDC

ALPHA IS THE NEW BETA

BETA

EVOLVING TO A SIGMA MINDSET Σ

DR CYRUS MARTIN

MIND FORGE PRESS

To my wife,
whose unwavering love, strength, and belief in me anchor my purpose—
and to our four incredible children,
who inspire me daily to lead with wisdom, grow with humility,
and evolve with love.
This is for you. Always.

© Cyrus Martin 2025
Mind Forge Press

ISBN: 979-8-9854706-8-0 Hardcover
ISBN: 979-8-9854706-9-7 Softcover
ISBN: 979-8-9997758-0-1 E-book
Audiobook

Library of Congress Control Number: 2025920789
Printed in the United States of America
First Edition

Book Design by Houston Creative Space

All names and identifying details in this book have been changed to protect the privacy and anonymity of individuals. Any resemblance to real persons, living or dead, is purely coincidental.

TABLE OF CONTENTS

Forward by Dr. Robert Hilliker 11
A Note from the Author 13
Introduction 17
   Why We Need to Move Beyond Labels 17
   Understanding the Tri-Sigma Approach 18
   Research Foundations 19
   How This Book Can Help 19
   How to Use This Book 20
   The Path Ahead 21
   A Personal Note 21
Chapter 1: What is the Tri-Sigma Approach? 23
Chapter 2: The Science of Mindfulness 37
Chapter 3: Professional Identity Formation 51
Chapter 4: Emotional Intelligence and Resilience 63
Chapter 5: Authentic Leadership 73
Chapter 6: Innovation and Adaptability 91
Chapter 7: Building Tri-Sigma Relationships 107
Chapter 8: Sustainable Success 119
Chapter 9: Future Professional Development 129
Conclusion: Integration of Key Ideas 139
   Action Steps for Readers 139
   Practice the Tri-Sigma Approach in Small Ways 140
   Resources for Further Growth 140
   Final Reflections 141
Endnotes 143
Appendices 145
   Appendix A: Research Methodology 145
   Appendix B: Mindfulness Exercises 146
   Appendix C: Professional Identity Assessment Tools 147
   Appendix D: Tri-Sigma as an Evolved State 147
Acknowledgements 151
About the Author 153

FORWARD BY DR. ROBERT HILLIKER

⋅╂────────────╂⋅

Over the years, I have had the privilege of working closely with Dr. Cyrus Martin—a colleague, collaborator, and friend whose professional path embodies the very principles he lays out in this book. In every meeting, case consultation, and program we've built together, I've witnessed his deep commitment to authenticity, mindful presence, and the development of a strong professional identity. These are not abstract ideals for Dr. Martin; they are the daily practices that shape how he engages with people, leads organizations, and approaches life.

Our shared work in the behavioral health field has given me a front-row seat to his integration of research and real-world practice. Whether navigating the complexities of organizational leadership or mentoring clinicians in the early stages of their careers, Dr. Martin models the "Tri-Sigma Approach" described in these pages—a way of leading and living that resists simplistic labels and instead embraces the full complexity of human potential.

One of the recurring themes in this book is the idea that growth is not linear, and that professional identity is not something we inherit from a title or role—it's something we shape through re-

ALPHA IS THE NEW BETA

flection, resilience, and an ongoing commitment to our values. In my years of collaboration with Dr. Martin, I've seen how his own journey reflects this truth. He meets challenges with flexibility, sees setbacks as opportunities for deeper learning, and keeps a steady focus on purpose over position.

Dr. Martin's research on mindfulness and professional identity as predictors of compassion satisfaction is more than an academic contribution—it's a lifeline for those of us in high-stakes, high-burnout professions. I have watched him bring these concepts to life in ways that strengthen teams, deepen clinical work, and sustain the very compassion that drew us to this field in the first place.

This book distills those insights into a practical, research-backed roadmap. It challenges us to move beyond the confining categories that often dominate professional culture, and instead build a more authentic, sustainable, and personally aligned way of working. If you engage with the exercises, stories, and strategies in these pages with the same openness and intentionality that Dr. Martin brings to his own practice, you will find not only tools for professional growth, but a framework for living and leading with integrity.

    Robert Hilliker, PhD, LCSW-S, LCDC
    Co-founder and Chief Clinical Officer
    Ethos Behavioral Health Group

A NOTE FROM THE AUTHOR

I sit down to write this book, reflecting on my early days as a counselor. Like so many helping professionals, I entered this career with great interest in helping others, but it wasn't without trepidation. In the beginning, I had the same issues that most helping professionals experience: how to remain compassionate without burning out, how to become a professional and still be me, and how to stay present in a mindful way despite this challenging work.

These challenges compelled me to study the role of mindfulness and professional identity in determining work satisfaction. In my study on counselors-in-training, here's what I know: where a strong professional identity is developed and mindfulness is practiced, we are better equipped to maintain the compassion that initially called us into the profession. But this book is not about the research findings. It's about real solutions for real people. As a practitioner with a thriving clinical practice, an executive leader in a non-profit housing organization, and parent of four, I know well the ever-present challenges of maintaining balance and finding fulfillment in our work.

The ideas in this book draw on my research and personal experience. I witness how a mindfulness practice helps me stay grounded

ALPHA IS THE NEW BETA

during times that are not easy. And I've watched counselors-in-training grow more confident as they developed their own mindfulness practice while also growing their identities as professionals. I witnessed how these elements worked together to assist us in maintaining compassion satisfaction—that sense in which we feel fulfilled from helping others. What has struck me throughout my career is how often we try to put ourselves and others into simple categories: alphas, betas—as if that in any way encompasses what it is to be human. These labels encumber and build boxes we must fit into in order to make it in the world. This book offers another direction, one which I'll call the Tri-Sigma Approach. It's an approach that takes the best of what I've learned through research and practice to help you:

- Establish a strong professional identity while being true to one's self
- Use mindfulness to stay present and engaged
- Maintain compassion and satisfaction even in the most difficult times
- Enjoy satisfaction in your career
- Find your own way to success beyond traditional labels

    You will find in this book practical exercises, stories from the field, and strategies that are backed by research. More importantly, you will find a roadmap for developing a mindset that will support both professional growth and personal wellbeing.

    I have written this book for all of the helping professions, including counselors, social workers, educators, organizational leaders, and all those who desire to make a difference while keeping their own wellbeing strong. Whether you're just starting out or a veteran in the field, I hope you find some tools and insights that resonate with your professional journey.

    As we embark on this adventure together, let me remind you

A NOTE FROM THE AUTHOR

humbly: this is not about trying to be someone you are not. It's about finding out who you already are and building on the strengths you've got inside. Instead, it's about ways of thriving professionally while remaining connected to what is important to you.

Let's move beyond partial and limiting labels that only take us so far, allowing us to see what is possible when we adopt a more complete view of professional development and personal growth. Welcome to your journey into the Tri-Sigma Approach.

Warmly,
Dr. Billy Cyrus Martin, PhD

ALPHA IS THE NEW BETA

INTRODUCTION

WHY WE NEED TO MOVE BEYOND LABELS

In the early days of my career, when attending one of those largely unremarkable leadership workshops that served to check a box, the presenter divided us all into two broad categories: Alphas and Betas. My colleagues visibly squirmed, their eyes widened in discomfort, trying to figure out which side of the room they'd claim. Those choosing the Alpha label wore their selection proudly, while the Betas looked almost apologetic. That moment stuck with me because it demonstrated how labels can make us feel superior or inferior, even if we're made uncomfortable by them.

Through years of research and current clinical practice, I have observed how these categories can affect self-worth and professional growth. These labels cannot fully represent our whole selves. They do not show our complexity, our potential, or the many ways our living in between labels makes valuable contributions to our fields and communities.

Let's talk about why these labels can be harmful. When we label someone an Alpha, we expect them to always be:

ALPHA IS THE NEW BETA

- Born leaders
- Confident
- Competitive
- Assertive

When we label someone a Beta, we assume they are:
- Followers
- Less confident
- Passive
- Unable to lead

But here's what I've found researching counselors and helping professionals: most of us do not fit squarely into just one of these categories. A strong therapist may be softly assertive in the counseling room but loud in team meetings. A capable leader might lean more towards collaboration instead of competition. These labels call for a choice between two binaries, but human nature is more complex.

UNDERSTANDING THE TRI-SIGMA APPROACH

Through my research on professional identity development, I've found that the most satisfied and effective professionals often operate outside these traditional categories. The Tri-Sigma Approach is about:

1. Self-Awareness
    - Understanding your unique strengths and challenges
    - Recognizing when to lead and when to support
    - Being honest about your needs and limitations

2. Flexibility
    - Adapting your approach based on the situation
    - Moving between different roles comfortably
    - Learning from every experience

INTRODUCTION

3. Authenticity
    - Being true to your values
    - Not forcing yourself into prescribed roles
    - Finding your own way to be effective

RESEARCH FOUNDATIONS

My doctoral research focused on how mindfulness and professional identity affect compassion satisfaction among helping professionals. Here's what I found:

1. Mindfulness Matters
    - Professionals who practice mindfulness report higher job satisfaction
    - Mindful awareness helps prevent burnout
    - Regular mindfulness practice strengthens professional identity

2. Professional Identity Development
    - A strong sense of professional identity increases confidence
    - Clear professional identity helps set healthy boundaries
    - Identity development is an ongoing process

3. The Connection to Satisfaction
    - Both mindfulness and professional identity predict job satisfaction
    - These elements work together to support professional growth
    - The combination helps maintain compassion and prevent fatigue

HOW THIS BOOK CAN HELP

Throughout this book, we'll explore practical ways to develop the

ALPHA IS THE NEW BETA

Tri-Sigma Approach. Each chapter includes:

1. Real Stories
    - Examples from my clinical practice
    - Experiences shared by research participants
    - Personal insights from my journey

2. Practical Exercises
    - Mindfulness practices you can start today
    - Professional identity development activities
    - Self-reflection prompts

3. Evidence-based Strategies
    - Practical approaches to professional growth
    - Tools for maintaining compassion satisfaction
    - Methods for preventing burnout

HOW TO USE THIS BOOK

This book is designed to be both a guide and a workbook. To get all that you can from it, I suggest active participation while you read and recommend:

1. Reading at Your Own Pace
    - Take time to reflect on each concept
    - Try out the exercises that resonate with you
    - Return to earlier chapters as needed

2. Journaling Your Journey
    - Keep notes about your insights
    - Track your experiences with the exercises
    - Document your growth over time

3. Applying the Concepts

INTRODUCTION

- Start with small changes in your daily routine
- Gradually incorporate more practices
- Adapt the strategies to fit your needs

THE PATH AHEAD

In the coming chapters, we'll explore:

1. Understanding your current approach
    - Identifying your strengths and growth areas
    - Recognizing limiting beliefs
    - Setting personal development goals

2. Developing Mindfulness Skills
    - Basic mindfulness practices
    - Professional applications of mindfulness
    - Building a sustainable practice

3. Strengthening Professional Identity
    - Clarifying your professional values
    - Building confidence in your role
    - Creating healthy boundaries

4. Integrating the Tri-Sigma Approach
    - Combining mindfulness with professional growth
    - Maintaining authenticity while developing skills
    - Finding your unique path to success

A PERSONAL NOTE

This book isn't about becoming someone else or fitting into some other category. It's about finding out who you already are and building a base from there. I have seen exceptional results from those

ALPHA IS THE NEW BETA

who take this approach.

My practice is filled daily with people striving to balance professional growth with personal authenticity. As a person who balances many roles myself—the clinician, the researcher, the executive, the parent—finding my place has been a very personal journey. Many of these strategies and insights form the backbone of this book.

In moving forward, remember that growth is not linear. Some days you will feel strong and confident, others you may question everything. That is normal; it's part of the process. The Tri-Sigma Approach isn't about reaching perfection; it's about continuous learning and development.

Let us begin this journey transcending some of these limiting labels with which we are burdened and work toward professional lives more in tune with ourselves. The path ahead isn't about becoming an Alpha, Beta, or even a Sigma—it's about becoming more fully yourself.

In the next chapter, we will begin by comparing the Tri-Sigma Approach with traditional approaches to professional development and explore why that is important to your growth and satisfaction at work.

CHAPTER 1: WHAT IS THE TRI-SIGMA APPROACH?

·┼─────────────┼·

I remember my first day as a counselor in training. Walking into that clinic, I felt the weight of expectations regarding how a counselor should comport themselves, speak, and even dress. I could see the unwritten hierarchy: at the top, senior counselors; in the middle, practitioners; and at the bottom, people like me, trainees. It was my first encounter with how professional hierarchies shape experiences and growth.

Having been in research and practice for these many years, I've seen personally how these structures of implied power impact people in helping professions. It is often the case with many of us that we enter these fields motivated by wanting to help others only to find ourselves entangled in systems that sometimes value rank over impact, position over purpose.

Let me illustrate this challenge with a story from my research. During one of my interviews, with a counselor I'll call Sarah[1], she identified traditional workplace hierarchies as one of the biggest battles she had to fight working for the agency. She had much to say that could help her clients, but she was "only a junior counselor" and did not feel she had anything of value to add to the treating of these clients. Her account reflects those of many professionals who must work

ALPHA IS THE NEW BETA

within hierarchical thinking that constrains both personal growth and organizational effectiveness.

It is here that we begin our discussion of the Tri-Sigma Approach—and how traditional hierarchies are often lacking. Here are three limitations of traditional hierarchical thinking: first, hierarchies often build artificial barriers. In working for nonprofit organizations, I've seen rigid hierarchies prevent good ideas from getting in front of decision-makers. When we think authority is coterminous with position, we are not taking advantage of valuable insights and innovations that can be created at any level in an organization.

Second, traditional hierarchies can harm professional identity development. In my research, professionals who were put into hierarchical boxes found it very difficult to develop an authentic professional identity, trying to fit their life into someone else's picture instead of developing their own path.

And third, hierarchical thinking impairs our compassion satisfaction—that sense of fulfillment we get when we feel our work has helped others. When we are too focused on position in the hierarchy, we lose track of why we chose this work in the first place.

Yet, moving beyond hierarchies does not mean we abandon structure in every form. Rather, we create more flexible and human-centered ways of working together. In my practice, the best teams are interconnected networks instead of rigid pyramids: each person brings unique experience and perspective, whatever their formal position may be.

Putting this human-centered structure into practice is not easy. I still remember a team of counselors who was totally dependent on the existing hierarchy paradigm. Initially, when we started introducing more collaborative approaches, some senior staff felt threatened. And junior members weren't sure how to step into new roles either. But over time, something quite remarkable took place: the team grew much more innovative, supportive, and ultimately effective in

CHAPTER 1: WHAT IS THE TRI-SIGMA APPROACH?

serving their clients.

The Tri-Sigma Approach affords us a different view of professional development and advancement. Instead of visualizing a ladder to climb, it invites us to reframe growth as multi-dimensional. Such thinking accords with what I've found in my studies on mindfulness and professional identity. Namely, professional development is much more than up-the-ranks promotion.

Let me give another example from my clinical practice. A mid-career client felt "stuck" in the hierarchy of his organization. As a function of our work together, he came to realize that his real growth wasn't moving up the corporate ladder but developing his permutation of skills and perspectives. This initially helped him find new satisfaction in work at a time when upward mobility was not feasible.

This movement beyond traditional hierarchies connects to my research on mindfulness and professional identity development. When professionals focus less on hierarchical position and more on authentic growth, my clients report higher levels of job satisfaction and resilience. Even more impressive, they report higher capacity for compassion.

This shift away from hierarchical thinking also influences how we understand success. Success within traditional hierarchies is often narrowly defined by position and power. But in studying counselors-in-training, we find that those who define success more broadly—by taking improvements in personal growth, impact on others, and work-life balance into consideration—tend to report higher levels of professional satisfaction.

That is not to say formal structures and roles of leadership have no importance. It suggests that it is time for a more nuanced understanding of how individuals contribute to organizations.

Reflect on your experiences with hierarchies through the course of your professional life. Were there any occasions when you felt confined to a certain position? How might hierarchical structures have curbed your capacity for growth and/or the feeling that you could make valuable contributions? How you answer these questions will be important for our discussion of the Tri-Sigma Approach.

Moving beyond hierarchies also means rethinking how we develop as professionals. Traditional hierarchies often specify one road to success. But my research shows that professional development is, in fact, inherently personal and hard to quantify. Each of us must find our own road to development and contribution, rooted in our unique strengths and values.

Incorporating a broader understanding of professional development is particularly important to helping professions as we tend to fall into the trap of thinking that a great deal of our effectiveness depends on our capacity to get ahead with the "right people." If we are too concerned with hierarchical position, then we may well overlook opportunities for much more powerful connections that could lead to a greater circle of influence. The Tri-Sigma Approach proposes that real professional development takes place in our lives when we:

- Focus on the development of our unique strengths rather than fitting into predetermined roles
- Value contribution and impact over position and rank
- Maintain authentic connections across organizational levels
- Make choices that align with our purpose and values
- Embrace lifelong learning and growth

In the following chapter, we'll detail the practical application of these principles. Further, we'll examine concrete ways to overcome hierarchical thinking without sacrificing professional effectiveness. It is a personal and professional journey beyond conventional hierarchies. The process invites questioning of our own assumptions about growth and success while remaining connected to our core purpose as helping professionals. We will discuss ways to adapt this more flexible and authentic approach to professional development.

CHAPTER 1: WHAT IS THE TRI-SIGMA APPROACH?

My insight into the core principles of the Tri-Sigma Approach began during one of the most challenging periods in my clinical practice. I was working with a group of counselors who were on the edge of burnout. I began to notice patterns in how some professionals managed to stay enthusiastic and effective at their work, while others struggled. One of these counselors—we'll call him Michael—still stands out in my mind. He'd been working for the past fifteen years. While many of his contemporaries had more traditional career development, Michael had forged his own path. "I stopped trying to be what others expected," he told me in our research interview. Instead, he learned about himself and how he could better help his clients. Michael's story illustrates the first core principle of the Tri-Sigma Approach: *self-awareness*.

In my investigation of mindfulness and professional identity, it has become clear that self-awareness is the foundation on which sustainable professional growth is built. Much more than merely identifying one's strengths and weaknesses, true self-awareness requires one to be vigilant in identifying their own patterns and triggers, as well as committed to searching out authentic ways of connecting with others. Personally, I've struggled with balancing my clinical practice, research, and family life. But I know that it is self-awareness that helps me make better decisions about how to use my energy, which leads to marked improvement in maintaining compassion satisfaction.

In working with veteran professionals, I found that those counselors who have the most compassion satisfaction have another guiding principle in common: they have very little concern for their position in traditional hierarchies. Their prevailing mindset is one of curiosity. I think of Maria, another research participant, saying, "Every encounter with a client is really an opportunity to learn anew. And after twenty years, I'm still growing." It is this continuous learning principle that keeps the work fresh and engaging.

My research indicates that professionals who embrace lifelong learning show higher levels of compassion satisfaction. For them, challenges represent opportunities for growth, not threats. It is this type of thinking that inhibits the stagnation that often precedes burnout.

Another core principle that crystallized through my work with counselors-in-training is the realization that forging authentic connections is paramount. Traditionally, in professional contexts, we maintain artificial barriers between ourselves and others. The Tri-Sigma Approach encourages appropriate, genuine connections while maintaining professional boundaries—an important balance for effectiveness and satisfaction.

I recall being in a group of new counselors who were struggling to find this balance. They had been taught to maintain strict professional distance, but by doing so they felt disconnected from their work. Through mindfulness practices and identity development work, they learned to bring more of their authentic selves into their professional roles while maintaining appropriate boundaries.

Another core principle that remains consistent across all the most satisfied of the research participants is that they all exhibited the character trait of *flexible resilience*. While rigid strength invites the undesirable possibility of breaking under pressure, flexible resilience enables us to confront and grow through challenges. Living through a global pandemic cast this into sharp relief. We witnessed time and again that the professionals who could adapt their approaches while holding onto their core values were better able to serve their clients.

One of the most powerful principles I observed is what I call purposeful presence. *Purposeful presence* calls us to bring mindfulness together with a clear professional purpose. Professionals who remain connected to their purpose—yet present in the moment—show higher levels of job satisfaction along with lower burnout rates.

There were times when I struggled between different roles: a researcher, a clinician, a parent. The Tri-Sigma Approach asks me to synthesize these roles into an integrated whole rather than to compartmentalize them. I learn that arriving at every moment in time without

CHAPTER 1: WHAT IS THE TRI-SIGMA APPROACH?

losing contact with the big picture allows me to juggle multiple responsibilities more effectively.

Staying in the Tri-Sigma Approach requires us to redefine success. Conventionally, success has been defined by events outside of one's control: promotions, awards, and outside recognition of status. But during my research, what worked for me was to learn that reframing my own definition of success more personally and holistically tends to sustain work satisfaction. I am reminded of a discussion that I had with a well-respected counselor. She was in a senior position, enjoyed professional acclaim, and had a thriving practice; still, none of that gave her as much satisfaction as the moments of true connection with her clients and younger professionals. Neither of these markers for "success" could be measured by her peers or her paycheck. Her story represents how the Tri-Sigma Approach encourages us to create our own personal definition of success.

The *integrated-growth principle* has set the tone in my work with counselors-in-training. Rather than seeing personal and professional growth as two divergent paths, the Tri-Sigma Approach invites us to see growth more holistically. This prevents the fragmentation that so often leads to burnout. When I started my doctoral research, I feared a potential trade-off between academic rigor on the one hand and practical relevance on the other. Adopting a Tri-Sigma Approach helped me understand how these seemingly disparate aspects of my work could reinforce one another rather than compete for my focus.

Another guiding principle that anchors the Tri-Sigma Approach is what I refer to as *compassionate boundaries*. The professionals most capable of sustaining their effectiveness over long periods of time are those who hold clear boundaries but remain compassionate—both with themselves and others. This is not about building walls; this is about creating healthy spaces for growth and connection.

The principle of *adaptive expertise* has been particularly helpful in today's fast-paced working environment. It is not just about acquiring knowledge, but about retaining the capacity for application of skills and knowledge in ways that may be different from how we were taught. This flexibility in conduct secures higher satisfaction in one's work life and over longer periods.

One particularly powerful principle I have seen in operation is what I call *authentic influence*. In contrast to traditional models of power—based on position or authority—authentic influence is rooted in true expertise, trustworthiness, and meaningful connection. This is a principle that will make a difference whether one is formally placed at a high or low level of authority. I have witnessed this transformation in my work in nonprofit leadership at the individual level but also organizational level. When people are empowered to work within their authentic strengths while being aligned with their shared purpose, the system as a whole becomes resilient and effective.

A final core principle I'd like to discuss, but not at all last in order of importance, is what I call *mindful evolution*. Mindful evolution recognizes that development is nonlinear and unpredictable; it's a continuing process of adaptation. Professionals who embrace this principle tend to maintain their enthusiasm and effectiveness even through challenging times.

In my research on professional identity development, I was looking for more than academic answers as I tested a series of questions that kept coming up for me. How do you help professionals develop a strong sense of professional identity and yet remain true to their person? What is it that prepares some to maintain their passion for their work while others burn out?

My doctoral research focused on counselors-in-training, but it applies to many folks in the helping professions. Here's what I found through both formal research and anecdotally though multiple years of clinical observation. One of my most memorable research participants was a counselor named James. He described the early struggle with professional identity: "At first I tried to copy my supervisors' styles

CHAPTER 1: WHAT IS THE TRI-SIGMA APPROACH?

exactly. It took me a while to realize that I needed to find my own way of doing this work."

James's experience illustrates what my research confirmed: professional identity is not something we can borrow from others. In studying hundreds of counselors-in-training, I found that professional identity develops through a combination of education, experience, and personal reflection. But more importantly, it develops best when we have space to integrate our personal values with professional requirements.

During my research interviews, I could sense in many participants a subtle pressure to fit into a mold. One participant reported, "I thought that for me to be professional, I needed to be serious at all times. Then I realized my natural sense of humor actually helped me connect better with clients." This constitutes an important insight from my research: authentic professional identity often develops when we stop trying to fit the mold of a stereotype.

The data emerging from the investigation indicates some interesting aspects of mindfulness and professional identity. Professionals who practice mindfulness on a regular basis self-report feelings of assurance in their professional role. Those who remain connected to their inner experience when learning a new skill are able to embrace developing their professional identity in a more effective way.

I fully lived this in my own professional identity development. Working on my PhD while running a clinical practice and raising four children often made me feel pulled in many different directions. The research I was conducting helped me understand that these different identities need not compete but could inform and enrich one another. A personal experience like this deepens my understanding of how professional identity develops in real-life settings.

One unexpected finding of my research was the positive role difficulty and discomfort plays in professional identity development. Hard times were commonly pointed to as important moments of growth. One participant shared with me, "It was actually during my biggest professional crisis that I really figured out who I was as a counselor." This fits for me with what I have observed through my clinical practice—our professional identity is often strengthened through challenges when we have the right support and mindset.

Another interesting pattern that this research unearthed was about compassion satisfaction; that is, that good feeling we get when we help others. It seems that professionals who have a strong sense of identity are able to maintain their compassion longer. They had much clearer boundaries and a better sense of their role.

I remember working with one group of new counselors from my research study who were entertaining the idea that they weren't yet "real" professionals. In other words, they were experiencing imposter syndrome. They learned, through our work together, that professional identity isn't some perfect destination, but rather a journey of continuous growth and development. This insight allowed them to relax into their roles and focus on learning, not proving themselves.

Professional identity development takes place through stages, not in a clear line. We do better when we think of it like the seasons: each person traverses similar phases at his or her own pace. Some may take a little more time in a stage; others may pass through it with remarkable rapidity.

It was perhaps most succinctly summed up by one savvy clinician when she said, "Some days, I feel completely confident in my work and professional role, and other days, I feel like I'm starting over from scratch. I've learned that's okay; it's growth." This type of insight has helped us better grasp that professional identity development is an ongoing, dynamic process, not a place at which we arrive.

Furthermore, I deduced that one's work in a community deeply influences professional identity. Inasmuch as individual reflection and practice are extremely important, we also need to have some connection with others in our professional lives. However, it is import-

CHAPTER 1: WHAT IS THE TRI-SIGMA APPROACH?

ant to say that those precious connections happen best when they are grounded in authenticity rather than hierarchy or a need to check off a required number of completed hours.

I've facilitated many supervision groups over time. Those groups that were the most effective were not the ones where I told people what to do; rather, they were groups where I established an environment where professionals could explore their dilemmas together, share their uncertainties, and help each other grow. This personal experience echoes my study participants: social impact of one's work community has great influence on professional identity development.

Another important finding arises from my study concerning the contribution of values to professional identity development. Those professionals who articulate their values clearly and link them to their work report greater job satisfaction and resilience. To be clear, this is not about the adoption of someone else's values; it is an understanding of how personal values enhance professional practice.

The research also shows interesting patterns in how professional identity develops differently in various settings: some participants work in very traditional hierarchical organizations, while others work in more flexible environments. Those working in more flexible settings often reported greater freedom to develop authentic professional identities, though they sometimes struggled with the lack of clear structures.

The development of professional identity for most participants eventually required establishing a reflective practice. Highly satisfied practitioners reported making purposeful and regular reflections a part of their regular practice. Professionals taking time out to reflect upon experiences, challenges, and growth were therefore more likely to have developed a stronger, more resilient professional identity.

I have committed to a similar practice on my own, as a researcher and clinician. Writing about experiences and relating them to broad patterns allowed me to deepen the understanding of my professional identity. This personal experience has helped me to understand the research data and help others develop their own professional identities.

Let me share a powerful moment that made me realize the deep connection between self-awareness, mindfulness, and professional growth. I was working with a group of healthcare workers who were overwhelmed. One of them said something that still rings clearly in my head. "I've been so focused on doing my job that I forgot to notice *how* I was doing it." It is this simple statement that truly underpins how self-awareness and mindfulness matter so much in our professional lives. Mindfulness is not just about finding a way to feel calmer but about developing a clearer understanding of ourselves and how we interact with others. Another research participant said it like this: "When I started practicing mindfulness, I began noticing patterns in how I responded to difficult clients. This awareness helped me make better choices in those moments."

In my daily life, the challenge presented by balancing clinical work, research, and family responsibilities taught me that self-awareness is not a luxury; it's an imperative. I remember days when I felt an urge to burrow under the load of meeting everyone's needs. Learning to stop and check in with myself helped me recognize how many times I needed to revise my approach or take time for self-care.

It is clear that professionals who practice mindfulness on a regular basis tend to sustain higher levels of compassion satisfaction. But what does this look like practically? For me, it means taking a few minutes between clients to breathe and reset. Sometimes it is as simple as paying attention to the sensation of my feet on the floor during a rough conversation. These momentary glimpses of awareness make a world of difference in how we show up in our work.

One interesting finding from my research involves how self-awareness prevents professional burnout: the more aware we be-

CHAPTER 1: WHAT IS THE TRI-SIGMA APPROACH?

come of our thoughts, feelings, and reactions, the more we can see signs of stress well in advance. I think of one counselor in my study who found herself becoming short-tempered with clients. Having developed keen self-awareness through mindfulness practice, she recognized this impatience as a sign not to be ignored. She had to act because she knew she was heading to burnout.

What really surprised me in the research findings is the role of mindfulness in professional identity development. The professionals who practice mindfulness felt more authentic in their roles: not just imitating mentors or following a set of rules, but developing their own style based on a deep understanding of themselves and of their values.

I worked with a new counselor who was struggling with confidence. After developing a regular mindfulness practice, she began to notice how her anxiety about "doing it right" was getting in the way of connecting with clients. This awareness helped her relax into a natural style, which made her a much more effective clinician.

Mindfulness doesn't just lead to more self-awareness in clinical practice. I also witnessed professionals who practice regular mindfulness react to difficulties with more flexibility and imagination. Instead of an automatic reaction, they can pause, assess the situation, and choose their response with much more thoughtfulness. When one has a deeper understanding of his or her own patterns and triggers—which can be intentionally developed through mindfulness practice—that person can communicate more clearly and set healthier boundaries. As one participant said, "Mindfulness helped me recognize when I was taking on a lot of my clients' problems. And now I can remain compassionate without becoming overwhelmed."

The connection between mindfulness and professional development is not just contained to the individual but extends to our interaction with others as well. Within my supervision groups, I see this pattern repeatedly: the clearer the development of self-awareness, the more receptive that clinician is in the face of feedback. These clinicians treat their supervisory sessions as an opportunity to learn from someone else's experience. Those steeped in a mindfulness practice are generally less defensive and more open to the opportunity that difficulties afford them.

Developing a mindfulness practice is no easy lift. Most of the participants in my research struggled with either finding the time or feeling they weren't "doing it right." What is important is that awareness cultivates a non-judgmental and steadfast balance that endures. In nearly all the professionals I have worked with or researched, I observed how self-awareness and mindfulness set the foundation for the Tri-Sigma Approach. With a greater awareness of self, we can begin to look beyond traditional hierarchies and authentically develop our professional identities. We can start recognizing our strengths and weaknesses as tools to help us break the molds we've created for ourselves.

In closing, let me stress that self-awareness and mindfulness are not destinations but a lifetime process. The practice reveals something new every day. Each day differs from others, and each opens up opportunities for growth in awareness. The Tri-Sigma Approach does not aim at attaining a perfect state of awareness, but rather we aim for a way of being in our professional lives that encourages continuous growth and authentic expression. We make space via self-awareness and mindfulness for this development to occur.

As you move forward on your journey, remember every small moment of awareness contributes to your professional growth. Whether you are at the start of your journey or have been practicing mindfulness for a long period of time, there is always more to understand and develop.

CHAPTER 2: THE SCIENCE OF MINDFULNESS

✦────────────✦

I naively thought, as I think most people do, that the definition of mindfulness was simple. Remain calm and get relaxed. But in researching the subject for my doctoral work, I realized my definition fell woefully short.

Let me start with a story from my clinical practice. Early in my career, I worked with a counselor named Rachel who struggled with the stress of the work. She said to me, "I keep hearing about mindfulness, but it seems too simple to really help with the heavy things we deal with in counseling." Her skepticism reflected what I think most helping professionals feel when they first encounter mindfulness. But what the research suggests—and what Rachel found out later—is that mindfulness can create real, quantifiable changes in how we think, feel, and work.

My research with counselors-in-training yielded some interesting results about mindfulness practices.[2] Those having regular practices in their lives reported not only feeling better but handling the tricky situations as successes. One of my participants describes it like this: "Before I started practicing mindfulness, I would get caught up in my clients' emotions. Now I can stay present with them while maintaining my own balance." I learned how mindfulness works at a number of important junctures: it helps us notice our thoughts and feelings without being overwhelmed by them. I interviewed several counselors who, since having taken up mindfulness regularly, report being able to notice when they are getting stressed or anxious without letting the feelings take over their work.

This research also yields surprising information about how mindfulness impacts our brains. Brain-scanning technology research has shown that regular mindfulness practices change the physical structure of the brain; namely it changes the part of the brain responsible for providing resources to manage stress, focus our attention, and feel compassion for others. You'll notice these are all essential skills for helping professionals.

This may play out in real situations. For instance, when practicing with a challenging client, my mindfulness practice turns my attention to noticing my reactions without interference in therapy. This again agrees with what the research suggests about mindfulness: it aids in regulating one's emotions.

One of the most critical findings from my research was about consistency in mindfulness practice. That is, it is not about having the most perfect, longest, distraction-free meditation sessions but rather regular, even brief, periods of mindful awareness. One counselor in my study began with just three minutes each morning of mindful breathing. Over time, her practice time increased and she became much more aware of her reactions throughout the day.

The research also illustrates how mindfulness helps us in ways we don't expect. To give just one example, studies have found that mindfulness boosts our immune system functioning and improves sleep. These physical benefits enable us to keep acting with compassion and effectiveness in our work.

I remember working with a group of health professionals who were very skeptical about mindfulness research. They wanted hard evidence that it would help them do their jobs better. So we looked

CHAPTER 2: THE SCIENCE OF MINDFULNESS

at studies showing how mindfulness improves attention and decision-making. An example of such a study included one that found that doctors who practice mindfulness make better diagnostic decisions and have better relationships with their patients.

Through my research interviews, I heard numerous stories about how mindfulness changed lives at work. As one counselor exclaimed, "I used to think that I was supposed to have an answer to all of the client's problems. Mindfulness has helped me learn my purpose is to be present and supportive, not to have an all-knowing attitude." This type of shift in perspective often creates better outcomes for professionals and their clients alike.

What intrigues me in this respect is how mindfulness seems to come in handy in different situations. Be it work stress, personal problems, or professional growth, mindfulness equips us with the wherewithal to cope more effectively. I find mindfulness improves my ability to juggle multiple responsibilities.

This study also points to something quite seminal about the effects of mindfulness on our interpersonal relations. Professionals who regularly practice mindfulness also tend to communicate better and be more empathetic. They're more able to pick up subtle cues from their clients and can sense when someone is holding back or needs extra support.

Perhaps the most specific mindfulness research finding that bears directly on helping professionals concerns its impact on compassion fatigue. Research concludes that a regular practice of mindfulness prevents burnout by enabling one to stay present in difficult situations and not feel overwhelmed—a powerful tool for any helping professional.

When teaching mindfulness to groups, I have ample opportunity to talk about both research findings and personal experiences: how even with short lengths of time, mindful breathing can decrease the stress hormones in our bodies. I see it for myself personally—if I have a busy clinic day, just a few mindful breaths between clients settles me down and keeps me focused.

The research also shows interesting patterns in how mindfulness skills evolve over time. It is not a linear process in which one is continuously getting better day by day. Rather, people often go through phases of insight followed by periods of integration. Understanding this helped me to be more patient, both with my own practice and with those I teach.

One counselor in my study described her experience this way: "Some days I feel very mindful and present; other days my mind is all over the place. The research helped me understand that this is normal—it's part of how our brains work." This kind of understanding helps people to stay committed to their practice even when it feels difficult. I still remember sitting in a conference room full of skeptical mental health professionals. One participant asked, "How do we know mindfulness actually changes anything in our brains?" This single questioner pointed me in the direction of one of the most fascinating parts of my journey: understanding how mindfulness affects our brain structure and function.

What scientists have discovered in the brains of people practicing mindfulness—through brain scanning technology—was a wonder to behold. In one such study, scans were performed on a group of people who had never tried any form of mindfulness practice. The brain scans of this cohort clearly showed physical changes in the brain after just eight weeks.

In my own clinical practice, I began to notice how such brain changes manifest in everyday life. I was seeing a counselor who had been practicing mindfulness for six months. She said to me, "I used to immediately react when clients would say something that was a trigger for me. Now, there's this tiny pause, and I have a choice in how I respond." This reinforces what the brain research tells us about how mindfulness strengthens our pause before we react.

CHAPTER 2: THE SCIENCE OF MINDFULNESS

In my doctoral research, it was clear that this understanding of brain changes helped people maintain a mindfulness practice. Understanding that they were literally reshaping their brains in helpful ways gave them motivation to continue. As one participant mentioned, "Knowing that each practice session was literally changing my brain made it feel more worthwhile, even on days when I didn't want to do it."

Changes in the brain don't just mean that people feel less impulsive. A regular practice impacts those parts of the brain involved in memory, emotional regulation, and decision-making. I noticed it in my life—once I had established the mindfulness practice, I found myself better able to remember details from client sessions and make clearer decisions under pressure.

Most exciting, in this regard, is the description of how mindfulness might affect our system related to the stress response. In our brain, there is an alarm system—the amygdala—which is activated every time we experience stress or danger. Research indicates that mindfulness practice reduces the size and activity of this alarm system while enhancing areas that facilitate staying calm and focused.

I watch this play out in my research with counselors-in-training. Those who continue to practice mindfulness regularly report feeling less overwhelmed by client emotions. Quite literally, their brains were becoming more resilient to stress. One participant said it was "like having a bigger container for difficult feelings."

What interests me more, however, is how such brain changes can affect our connectedness with others. There is evidence that mindfulness enhances parts of the brain involved in empathy—that is, understanding of the emotions of others. In my clinical supervision groups, it is clear that counselors who practice mindfulness regularly are more sensitive to their clients' needs.

If we consider neuroplasticity—or how the physical processes of the brain change with learning—we learn our brains continue to adapt and grow through life. Mindfulness exploits this ability for better attention, emotional awareness, and stress management. As one savvy counselor explained, "It was like upgrading my brain's operating system."

Mindfulness strengthens certain parts of the brain, just as physical exercise does for our muscles. When I teach counselors-in-training about brain changes and mindfulness, I use the analogy of exercise. When we exercise our bodies regularly, we achieve greater levels of stamina and heart health. I heard many stories of how these brain changes affected clients' ability to stay focused on everyday tasks for longer periods. One counselor said to me, "I used to get mental fatigue after a few client sessions. Since starting mindfulness practice, extended periods of time can pass while I remain focused and present." This parallels research that shows the way mindfulness reflects our brain's ability to sustain attention.

What's especially encouraging about this rapidly growing area of brain research is that real benefits occur even after small doses of practice. In my own life, I couldn't always find time for long meditation sessions. But research has shown that even short, regular practices can lead to positive brain changes. I still remember a particularly busy group of healthcare workers who insisted they had no time for mindfulness. When I presented research that just five to ten minutes a day could change the functioning of their brains, they were decidedly more open to giving it a try. Many months later, they said they noticed real and positive changes in how they coped with work stress.

Mindfulness further affects even how we process our emotions by changes that occur in the brain. Evidence does show strengthening in areas that could help a person understand their feelings. As I studied, I noticed that the professionals who were mindful were always better at taking stock of their emotional state and making intentional, less reactive choices.

One surprise arising out of the neuroscience research is how

CHAPTER 2: THE SCIENCE OF MINDFULNESS

mindfulness changes our sense of self. Changes in areas linked to self-reference and self-awareness show up on brain scans. I saw this reflected in my research participants: they often reported that, after they had developed a regular practice, they felt more connected both to themselves and others.

My experience supervising beginning counselors has taught me that an understanding of these brain changes helps individuals to trust the process of mindfulness. When they are aware there is significant science behind the practice, they are more likely to continue the practice through those tough early stages. One supervisor shared, "Knowing my brain was actually changing helped me keep practicing when I wasn't seeing effects."

Through years of research and clinical work, I'm never not pleasantly surprised by what happens at the intersection of mindfulness and professional development. I specifically recall a discussion where this lens clicked into place for me. Working with a cohort of incoming counselors, one shared this particularly resonant sentiment: "I thought mindfulness was just about feeling peaceful, but it's actually helping me become a better counselor."

This observation is consistent with what I have learned from counselors-in-training. Those who practice mindfulness on a regular basis don't just feel calmer, but they also find that they develop professional skills more rapidly. One participant explained: "When I'm more mindful, I catch things in therapy sessions that I might have missed before. I notice small changes in my clients' expressions, tone of voice, even the way they sit."

Through my own journey combining research and clinical work, I noticed how rooted mindfulness is in the process of professional development. Thus, at the beginning of teaching others out in the field, mindfulness helped me to become aware of students' struggles that were not overtly expressed. That kind of awareness usually takes years to develop, but mindfulness seems to have sped up the process for me.

In my doctoral research, I learned that mindfulness serves professional development in a number of key ways. First, it improves our ability to learn from experience. When we're being more mindful, we pay greater attention to what is going on in our work, what's working well, and what needs adjustment. This happened with a counselor in my study who started keeping a mindfulness journal of her sessions. She learned more from each client interaction because she was paying better attention.

I saw a greater interrelationship between mindfulness and professional growth as I reviewed how it directly impacted supervision. Mindfulness-practicing counselors benefit more from their supervision sessions, recall interactions with their clients better, and receive feedback more positively. As one supervisor said to me, "The mindful trainees seem to learn faster because they're really present during the supervision, not just waiting for their turn to talk."

I reflect on my experience as the supervisor of counselors over the years: those who receive training in the skills of mindfulness often seem to demonstrate a different quality of professional growth—they are not just learning techniques; they are coming to a deeper understanding of themselves and their work. And that does accord with what research tells us about mindfulness enhancing self-awareness and emotional intelligence.

The research finding that intrigues me the most is how mindfulness enables people to deal more constructively with professional challenges. Professionals who were more mindful were better at weathering difficult situations without being overwhelmed. A counselor in my study described working with a particularly challenging client: "Before mindfulness, I would have gotten caught up in their anger. Now I can stay present and helpful without losing my own balance."

The impact of mindfulness upon professional confidence has been fascinating to watch. What I've come to realize is that people who

CHAPTER 2: THE SCIENCE OF MINDFULNESS

practice mindfulness regularly develop a different type of professional confidence. It's not about knowing all of "the rules;" rather, it's about being comfortable with uncertainty and grounded in your skills and knowledge. I will never forget the group of seasoned counselors that undertook a mindfulness practice together and spoke about how their counseling practices seemed new again—as if they were viewing their clients with fresh eyes. One said to me, "I thought after twenty years I knew it all about counselling. Mindfulness showed me that there's always something to learn."

Mindfulness has enabled me, in my professional development, to balance the variety of roles I've undertaken—researcher, clinician, supervisor, and parent. It makes me more aware when I am pulled this way or that and when a readjustment is called for. This level of awareness is important for sustainable professional development.

This is related to professional creativity in an intriguing way: when we are more mindful, we easily develop the ability for flexible thinking. I saw this with a counselor who had been stuck in a rigid way of working; through mindfulness practice, she was starting to find new ways of helping her clients.

One of the many aspects in which mindfulness supports professionals is by strengthening emotional resilience. The findings support that professionals who practice mindfulness on a regular basis manage job stress better and maintain their enthusiasm for work. One participant summed it up like this: "Mindfulness helps me remember why I chose this work in the first place."

I have noticed in my supervision groups that the people who practice mindfulness set much better professional boundaries. When we tune into our thoughts and feelings, we know when stepping back would be in order. Such self-awareness is key to long-term well-being in professional life.

I have found the relationship between mindfulness and ethical practice particularly pronounced. Mindful professionals seem to make ethical decisions thoughtfully, being aware of their biases and considering different perspectives more carefully. I once heard a counselor comment, "Mindfulness helps me notice when my personal feelings might be affecting my professional judgment."

During times of stress in my practice, lessons from unexpected times in the past help to guide me through. My experience as a young violinist in the Houston Youth Symphony endowed me with a kind of discipline that continues to this day. Fourteen years of classical training spent rehearsing scales and perfecting pieces taught me about the management of stress: consistent, dedicated practice.

My life path has not been linear; in high school, I juggled extra practice sessions on the violin with delivering pizzas for an italian restaurant and caterer where I learned my first lessons in serving the public. The owner is a friend to this day. His years teaching me to find meaning in any job precipitated a life-long friendship. Much later, while waiting tables at another of his restaurants, these lessons in human connection and dogged determination were further cemented.

Creative expression has been invaluable in helping me process the difficulties of life. I channeled this into architecture in high school, winning first place in a state competition in which I designed and built an extremely detailed scale model of a home. This experience taught me the value of careful planning and precise execution—skills that later became indispensable in my counseling career.

At the tender age of nine, the divorce of my parents could have made me bitter; instead, it taught me about resilience. While they divorced, I never had any of the feelings of conflict usually experienced by the children of divorce. I maintained a very close relationship with my dad. Through this, I came to realize how the challenges thrown at us by life need not be burdens that define us; we can always choose our response.

My twenties took me along the path of professional audio engineering in Austin and Atlanta. The music industry did bring excite-

CHAPTER 2: THE SCIENCE OF MINDFULNESS

ment and close friendships with it, but it also exposed me to a darker side of life that eventually caught up with me. I spent much of my time in recording sessions, mixing tracks with just about anybody, and spent just as much time questioning if this was really my calling. I enjoyed the technicality and attention to detail attendant with audio producing, but something was missing: the human connection.

It was during this reflective time that I knew I had to continue with my education and become a counselor. It would be different this time, unlike the earlier academic experiences that had brought me to this point. I dove into my studies with an enthusiasm that I had never known. Success in the program wasn't about good grades but finding my true path.

These diverse experiences have molded my methods of dealing with stress and assisting others. The discipline of musical training, the human connections from service jobs, the precision of architectural design, and the creative expression of audio engineering all fit together in a sort of biographical scaffolding that helps me face present-day difficulties.

I try to share with stressed clients how the background in music helped me understand the importance of practice and patience. Just as a violin concerto is mastered through constant effort every day, the skill of managing stress needs time and nurturing. It was the precision architectural design that taught me to take seemingly insurmountable situations and break them into manageable components. The skills I learned as an audio engineer—listening carefully, paying attention to the nuances, finding harmony in discord—now serve me during counseling sessions. Sometimes, helping someone out of a crisis is a lot like mixing a complicated track. You're trying to balance all these elements and maintain the clarity and integrity of the artist's vision. Getting married at thirty-nine taught me quite late that everybody is running at different timelines. This thought helps me to consider those clients who feel pressure from society. Life isn't about racing to meet arbitrary deadlines; life is about finding your rhythm and tempo.

It was always in the music that I found my solace and means of expression. The discipline from classical training informs how I structure may approach to overcoming challenges. Be it navigating my own personal stress or helping clients through their own stressors, the same core principles see us through: practice, patience, and perseverance.

What I have learned in life on this journey is that in order to manage stress, there is no single approach. Just like a musician building a repertoire, or an engineer fine-tuning a mix, every experience adds yet another instrument in my orchestra of coping strategies.

Anna was a counselor I'd been helping and the first person to bring up the idea of mindfulness to me. "It might help you manage the anxiety," she said one evening after my having complained about a particularly bad day. I was skeptical at first, being a pragmatic person accustomed to acting rather than reflecting. It seemed that all that sitting still and concentrating on breathing was a little too passive for me to believe it'd be useful.

But necessity is not just the mother of invention. Turns out she's a great teacher too. On one of my many visits to the clinic where I was interning, a gentle therapist there introduced me to my first real mindfulness exercise.

"Close your eyes," she said, sitting beside my desk. "Just focus on your breathing. Don't try to change it—just notice it." Her voice was soft, steady. "When your mind wanders to worry about symptoms or the future, just bring it back to your breath."
Easier said than done, of course. My mind immediately kicked into high gear, thinking of all the problems I had yet to sort out: bills, upcoming tests, work apprehensions. But little by little, I learned to appreciate the beauty in such moments of quiet. I moved from skeptic to mindfulness practitioner. I established a routine every morning:

- Five-minute quiet breathing before getting out of bed

CHAPTER 2: THE SCIENCE OF MINDFULNESS

- Gentle body scanning to check for any new symptoms
- Writing in my journal without judgment
- Setting minor, achievable goals for the day

These simple practices helped me stay connected to the present moment when everything else seemed out of control. During anxiety attacks, I found myself paying attention to my senses. It's a mindfulness practice I also share with my clients to help them calm their own senses in the midst of such attacks.

- Five things I can see
- Four things I can touch
- Three things I can hear
- Two odors I can smell
- One thing I can taste

This technique became my anchor during challenging moments. It was of great help at the clinic when the environment was overwhelming.

An unlikely contributor to my mindfulness practice came in the person of a former intern colleague named Marco. He began sending me short recordings of his daily journal check in: the morning sun on the buildings, the yeasty smell of fresh bread from a bakery down the street, and the sound of church bells. These audio entries became a regular feature of my daily meditation, a bridge to the world outside my work.

I also learned to eat mindfully. Every meal was an opportunity to exercise active awareness.

- Checking ingredients carefully
- Noticing textures and temperatures
- Eating more slowly and mindfully
- Monitoring the reactions of my body

ALPHA IS THE NEW BETA

I learned to open my days with a "body weather report" system. Every morning, I would check in with myself:

- How is my energy?
- What is my level of pain?
- How is my breathing?
- Am I experiencing new symptoms?
- How is my emotional state?

This systematic approach to mindfulness training resonated with my therapeutic education. It allowed me to better articulate any concerning symptoms to my doctors and to track patterns in my condition. I also learned to find moments of quiet in unexpected places. These precious minutes, which in the early days of my mindfulness practice I'd perceived as a waste of time, now became opportunities for practice and reflection. I started keeping a separate journal, just for mindfulness observations.

- What practices help most on difficult days?
- How does each technique affect my symptoms?
- Are there ways to modify exercises when I'm not feeling well?
- Do I notice any emotional patterns and triggers?

The journal that came out of this practice became a treasured asset, and not just to me. I wrote what I felt in uncomplicated language, free from medical jargon and complex instructions. I shared it with others who might see some of their own challenges reflected in mine.

CHAPTER 3: PROFESSIONAL IDENTITY FORMATION

❖────────────❖

I learned what professional identity truly means during an unplanned moment early in my counseling career. Sitting with my client, drawing on my classical music training to listen for subtle changes in their tone of voice, I realized my past experiences were not at war with my counselor role; they were enhancing it. It was a moment that helped me realize professional identity is not about becoming someone new; it is about integration. It's the perfect union of who we are *with* what we are.

In my research with counselors-in-training, I have witnessed how many labor to define their professional identity. As one participant related to me, "I thought I had to leave my old self behind to become a 'real' counselor." This construct of choice between our personal and professional selves comes up all the time. In my own trajectory from musician to audio engineer to counselor, each new role has added layers rather than replaced what came before. The discipline I learned as a violinist, the technical precision from engineering, the human connections from service jobs—all these experiences shape how I work with clients today.

A key takeaway of my doctoral research was crystallizing my understanding of professional identity as that which can only develop over the course of many years. It is the cumulative effect of education, experience, and personal reflection, and it is unique to the individual. Just as every life path is different, professionals bring their own individual background, values, and strengths to their work.

I recall supervising one counselor who was worried that her previous career as a schoolteacher might get in the way of her work as a counselor, that she might not be able to fully switch to counselor mode. As it turned out, her teaching background continued to bring a special perspective to working with families and children. This is a good example of how professional identity is often developed by building bridges between our past and present experiences.

A strong professional identity is built in phases. Specifically, for those in the helping profession, we first become grounded in knowledge: theories, modalities and techniques, and ethical guidelines. Second, we integrate that knowledge with our personal belief system. We ask, where does this knowledge fit into our values and experience base? Again, I go back to that high school architecture competition to construct my own building design and how it taught me to see both the details and the big picture—a skill that helps me to this day in case conceptualization.

One of the biggest takeaways from my research was how professional identity impacts job satisfaction. When professionals have a clear idea of who they are at work, there is more fulfillment and less burnout. I know this firsthand. When I transitioned from the music industry to counseling, I found a vocation consonant with my values and one that integrated skills I had already begun to develop. Everything seemed to matter so much more.

In interviews, many of the counselors-in-training spoke anxiously about "finding their style." Many strived to perfectly mimic their supervisors; perhaps they thought that this was the way to "sound" more professional. However, the research firmly suggests that professional identity is most authentic when we learn to marry professional

CHAPTER 3: PROFESSIONAL IDENTITY FORMATION

knowledge with the natural way we are. I think back to my own journey of discovery as I learned how my musician's ear helped me pick up on subtle emotional cues during therapy sessions.

Professional identity also means placing in perspective the part we play within the greater practitioner community. As a late starter in the counseling field, I assumed this meant I was somehow trailing behind in some imaginary race. Research and experience teach me, however, that having many life experiences across a wide range of professional environments enhances rather than detracts from professional identity.

The process of refining one's own professional identity does not always follow a smooth trajectory. Indeed, uncertainty and self-doubt are common experiences among my research participants. One counselor recounted her confusion in trying to balance her naturally warm personality against what she regarded as "professional distance." She discovered through supervision and personal reflection that her warmth is actually a professional strength when intentionally balanced with the setting of appropriate boundaries.

Professional identity, much like playing an instrument, advances through stages. Just like mastering an instrument, it takes time. So many new counselors become frustrated by what they perceive as a slow process. One such counselor lamented, "I feel like I should know exactly who I am as a counselor by now." It reminded me of my journey, not just in counseling but in my earlier career as an audio engineer. Each profession taught me that identity development happens gradually, in layers.

It often begins with what I refer to as "trying on the role." I see this again and again with counselors-in-training. They tend to mirror their supervisor's style, even down to their supervisor's mannerisms or phrases. I did this myself when I first started—it's the same as playing scales when you first begin the violin. It's not until much later that you have the ability to interpret a musical piece during performance. As one respondent eloquently summed up, "I felt like I was wearing someone else's clothes. They fit okay, but they weren't really mine." This stage is an important one, though. It provides a foundation from which to build. Even my restaurant job taught me the basics of customer service; I depended on experienced servers to show me the ropes until I could find my own style.

After we get comfortable in our own clothes, we come to what I refer to as "the wobble." We start to assiduously doubt everything we thought we knew. I found this stage to be fairly universal in my research. First you learn the basic rules of architecture, then you have to learn when and how to break them creatively. One participant in my study describes this stage like this: "At times I would feel confident, but at other times I would feel that I should transfer into a different profession altogether." It reminded me of my transition from the music world into counseling. The uncertain phase can be an uncomfortable place to be, yet it usually precedes growth.

Next is the integration stage, where we start to meld our professional knowledge with our personal style. At this stage, things start to feel more natural. For me, it came at the point when I started bringing my musical training into my counseling work: using my ear for subtle changes in tone and rhythm to pick up on clients' emotional shifts.

This is often a stage where confidence increases. One counselor described this as "finally finding my voice." It's a feeling of winning, a memorable point where reaching technical mastery intersects with personal creativity.

Finally, if we're fortunate, we come to the refinement phase. This is when further growth continues from a more stable base. I reflect upon my marriage at age thirty-nine—how waiting enabled me to bring more maturity and self-knowledge to that relationship. Professional identity follows a similar development trajectory. As one of my research participants said, "I'm still learning and growing, but now it

CHAPTER 3: PROFESSIONAL IDENTITY FORMATION

feels like *adding* to who I am rather than trying to *figure* out who I am."

What interests me most along this continuum is how these stages are not strictly linear. We might feel quite satisfied with our professional identity only to find ourselves thrown into circumstances that make us question it all over again. I have found this myself in making the transition from audio engineering to counseling; the skills I thought I was leaving behind—careful listening and technical precision—ended up being useful in many unexpected ways.

Personal life events can also have profound and unexpected effects on the development of professional identity. For example, it could be my parents' divorce when I was nine years old that shaped my drive to explore family dynamics. These experiences not only influence our professional identity but also become part of it.

Another finding that emerged in my research is the influence of cultural and personal background on stages of professional development. One counselor who participated in my study explained how her immigrant background made her initially feel like an outsider within the profession. Moving through the various stages of identity development, she began to see her background and the unique perspective it grants her as one of her most valuable strengths.

I came to understand the affiliation between professional identity and career satisfaction when transitioning from audio producing into counseling. I was satisfied with all of my technical abilities in recording studios, but something didn't seem to fit quite right. It wasn't until I finally found my professional identity as a counselor that I realized just how strongly job satisfaction is tied to knowing who we are at work.

In my studies with counselors-in-training, themes emerged reflecting how professional identity relates to career satisfaction. One story lingers with me. One participant in my study worked competently in the corporate sector for many years but complained of feeling unfulfilled. Upon entering counseling as a profession, she said, "For the first time I feel like my work is an expression of who I am, not just what I can do."

It also reflects my own experience with music: those fourteen years of classical violin training taught me that possessing technical skills alone does not engender satisfaction. What matters is how we link those skills with our sense of self. I see it so clearly now in my counseling practice. The days when I feel the most satisfied are those when I am fully expressing my professional identity, bringing along all parts of my experience.

I found that the participants who bring all of their values, strengths, and past life experiences to bear in their professional roles tend to feel more satisfied with their jobs across various indicators. They reported being more confident in decision-making processes, more authentic in relationships, and more resilient in the face of challenges. One counselor described it as "finally working from my center rather than trying to meet everyone else's expectations."

When I analyzed the variance of burnout rates, it crystallized the connection for me that professional identity has with career satisfaction. Professionals not possessing a grounded sense of identity tried to be all things to all people, struggled with setting and maintaining boundaries, and were generally drained by their work. I remembered waiting tables where servers who knew their style and strengths would enjoy their work more than others who were stuck still trying to please everybody.

My research also made me understand how professional identity influences the way we approach challenges at work. When we know who we are professionally, we can make better decisions on which opportunities to take and which to let go. I learned this lesson during my architectural competition in high school: success came not from trying to copy others' styles but from developing my own approach.

It is during periods of change when this relationship between identity and satisfaction becomes crucial. I reflect on how my marry-

CHAPTER 3: PROFESSIONAL IDENTITY FORMATION

ing late has been so satisfying to me, having waited for the right time, after I had truly come to know myself. Similarly, a solid professional identity helps people navigate through job changes with more success.

Another insight I take from this research is the power of a strong professional identity to mediate our relationships with colleagues and clients. Those who have clearly developed their professional identity are able to establish more genuine relationships and stronger collaboration. It reminds me of friendships that I formed in my pizza delivery days: the best work relationships came from just being myself, not some mold that I was expected to fit into.

Another finding reveals that professional identity affects how we handle feedback. When we're secure in our professional identity, feedback becomes an opportunity for growth, not a threat to our competence. I saw this in my violin training; once I developed confidence in my own musical voice, I could learn from criticism without feeling diminished by it.

Having supervised numerous counselors over the years, I have become very aware of how the process of developing a professional identity impacts job longevity. Those who develop a strong sense of who they are within their role do seem to last longer and find more satisfaction in their work. One of the participants in my study put it this way: "Once I stopped trying to be 'the Perfect' and started being myself as a counselor, everything got easier."

The effect of professional identity on career satisfaction further extends to how we deal with stress. In the research that I conducted, professionals who strongly identify with their work show more potential to manage their well-being even when times get tough. They have clearer boundaries and more appropriate self-care practices. It reminds me of how developing the discipline to study music for so many years as a young person helps me structure my work life to this day.

Professional identity influences our capacity for self-advocacy as well as that of our clients. We will be in a position to have our say when the time comes since we know who we are and what we stand for as professionals. My experience across several careers endows me with the confidence to stand firm in my values.

We would do well to take this confident approach when it comes to professional growth. Those individuals who have a well-defined sense of identity are more likely to choose development opportunities that better match their values and strengths, thus leading them to more satisfying careers. I have experienced this in my journey. Rather than each being a fresh start, somehow the steps from music to counseling to research built one upon the other.

A strong professional identity influences our experience of success. Rather than taking their cue from external measurements, professionals who have developed a strong sense of identity create their own markers of success. Consequently, they enjoy more enduring satisfaction. One counselor in my study said, "I used to think success meant having all the answers. Now I know it's about being fully present and authentic with my clients."

A strong sense of one's professional self carries over into career satisfaction and how we manage professional relationships. When we are secure in our professional identity, we can do our job in collaboration without feeling threatened by others' success. Through research and personal experience, I have seen how professional identity influences the capacity to sustain passion for our work over long periods of time.

Individuals who hold a strong sense of identity find ways to keep their work fresh and engaging even after many years in the field. They continue to grow yet remain steadily true to the core of their professional self. We have more capacity to mentor others. The more secure we are in our professional identity, the more we are able to support others in developing theirs. This has deeply influenced my approach to supervision, making space for each individual to develop

CHAPTER 3: PROFESSIONAL IDENTITY FORMATION

his or her own professional voice.

Creating an authentic professional presence is similar to my experience playing the violin with the Houston Youth Symphony. Just as each musician must find their unique voice while blending in harmony with the orchestra, so must a counselor develop their own counseling style while learning how to effectively work with others.

In my research, authentic professional presence was repeatedly self-reported as being directly linked to understanding one's own personal story. One such counselor reflected on how, early in her career, she did not disclose her background as a teacher, believing it made her appear less professional as a counselor. She came to understand and appreciate how her teaching experience gave her a unique perspective on human development and learning—and in fact, contributed to her effectiveness as a counselor.

My own varied career path taught me about authentic presence. Indeed, I learned about technical precision and attention to detail in recording studios. And these skills did not disappear when I became a counselor; instead, they morphed into careful attention to client narratives and subtle emotional shifts. This is a lesson: authentic presence means integrating—rather than hiding—our past experiences.

One of the most memorable moments in research was when a counselor tried to explain her struggle with professional presence. She self-reported, "I kept acting serious because I thought that is what professionals do. Then I realized that my natural warmth and humor helped clients feel comfortable." Her story illustrates a realization common to many counselors—authenticity serves us better than trying to fit into an expected professional mold. The connection between authentic presence and best practices came alive for me in my doctoral research: practitioners who bring their whole selves to work report improved client relationships and outcomes. It's similar to my experience as a food delivery driver: the real contact with customers nightly made the work both more rewarding and effective.

ALPHA IS THE NEW BETA

The emergence of authentic presence also involves recognizing our difficulties and areas for growth. In my supervision groups, I ask counselors to be transparent about their doubts. When done in a professional way, such openness actually enhances, rather than diminishes, one's credibility. I first came to understand this while participating in architectural competitions in high school—displaying my design process including the mistakes and revisions—made my final presentation more riveting.

The authentic professional presence that I've adopted over many years in the field was developed through conscious practice, rather like the development of my violin skills. In fact, authentic presence requires steady reflection and intentional growth. For example, one of the counselors who participated in my study kept a professional journal about times when she felt the most and least authentic. This practice helped her find her true professional style.

A counselor's own cultural background certainly plays a role in authentic presence. I found several practitioners who recalled feeling they needed to repress cultural identity early on in their practice so they wouldn't appear unprofessional. The confidence that comes with experience allowed them to bring their cultural perspective into the workplace and to make their practices more effective, serving clients of different backgrounds.

Authentic presence also involves knowing how to adjust one's style while being true to oneself. While a young waiter, I learned to adapt to various customers' approaches while remaining true to myself. Though the setting is very different, these same skills can be applied in the therapeutic setting as well, where we are always asked to meet differing client's needs while maintaining an authentic presence.

What surprised me in the research, though, was the effect authentic presence had on collegial relationships. Professionals who develop authentic presence reported better connections with colleagues and more satisfying mentoring relationships. That makes me think of

CHAPTER 3: PROFESSIONAL IDENTITY FORMATION

close friendships formed in my music training that have lasted, based as they are on authentic interaction rather than professional posturing.

Authentic presence is about being courageous. So many research participants talked about a moment of vulnerability in relationships with colleagues, where one would choose to be genuine rather than hiding behind professional distance. These became moments of breakthrough connection. The study also reveals how authentic presence affects our ability to navigate challenging situations in the workplace. In this way, when we are authentically present as professionals, we can more easily navigate challenging moments. One counselor explained that being authentic about her own journey in recovery—even while making sure to maintain appropriate boundaries—served to connect to her clients when they struggled with similar issues.

It means that the development of authentic presence all depends on balancing professional standards and personal style. Those professionals who are able to find this balance in their professional work report better job satisfaction and improved client outcomes. It's like exploring your unique musical interpretation while staying true to the composer's intentions.

Time and experience breed real presence, but it's not inevitable. I have found that reflecting deeply on one's practice matters more than years of experience. As we conclude the discussions in this chapter on professional identity formation, remember that authentic presence is something that unfolds over time. Much like my fourteen years of training on the violin provided a lifelong musical foundation, our professional identity and authentic presence are developed over the course of long, fruitful careers. The important part is that we remain true to ourselves as we grow professionally.

ALPHA IS THE NEW BETA

CHAPTER 4: EMOTIONAL INTELLIGENCE AND RESILIENCE

Working at a state-sponsored intensive outpatient clinic early in my career helped me cultivate a stronger grasp of emotional intelligence. What I learned about working with people who generally did not want to be there—CPS cases, DWI cases, and unhoused people—was that it wasn't just about drawing on book knowledge; rather, if I was going to succeed in this role, I needed to forge a deeper connection with these clients.

I'll never forget one especially tough day at the clinic: a CPS-mandated client came in angry and resisting treatment. My training had taught me protocols and procedures, but emotional intelligence allowed me to observe the fear beneath his anger. Instead of reacting to hostility, I observed his emotional place, waded into the waters where he was, and adapted my approach. This was my first practical application of the Tri-Sigma Approach: observe, accept, adapt.

In my trajectory from Director of Admissions to Vice President of Operations at a large behavioral health company, I have seen how emotional intelligence shapes leadership. Those who mentored me were not just technically proficient but knew and understood the human side of behavioral health. They taught me that less arbitrarily discursive thinking and more action accompanied by emotional awareness leads to truly effective leadership.

One experience during my time as director stands out. A staffer who was suffering from serious burnout had grown irritable, and his job performance was declining. Instead of jumping to disciplinary action, I took time to observe the situation fully. It wasn't that his skills were evaporating, or that he was growing defiant. What I saw instead was someone dealing with compassion fatigue. By accepting this rather than fighting it, we could adapt our approach to find solutions that helped both the staff members and our clients.

The transition across executive life into private practice and now back into the leadership role with an affordable housing non-profit has taught me something important about emotional intelligence: it is not about understanding emotions but taking that understanding and using it to create meaningful action.

Many people misunderstand the term emotional intelligence. They equate someone with a high EQ as someone who never loses their temper and always suppresses negative emotions. In my work with extremely diverse populations—from mandated clients to corporate executives—I've come to understand that emotional intelligence means being real about emotions: to meditate rather than contemplate, to observe rather than react. I developed the Tri-Sigma Approach over years of observing what really works when lives are at stake. Later, as I transitioned from clinical work into executive leadership, the same principles still very much applied. Whether with a resistant client or a challenging board meeting, the key was first to observe without judgment, accept the reality of the situation, and then adapt the approach accordingly.

As vice president, I remember one case where we were making a significant change in treatment protocols and were experiencing significant resistance from staff members. Using the Tri-Sigma Approach, I decided not to reactively push harder against resistance.

CHAPTER 4: EMOTIONAL INTELLIGENCE AND RESILIENCE

Instead, I first observed the true sources of the staff's concern and accepted that their concerns were valid instead of dismissing them. Ultimately, we adopted an implementation plan to take into consideration these concerns while reaching our goals.

I have seen keen emotional intelligence play a pivotal role in navigating the affordable housing landscape. The abilities developed through work with mandated clients in our outpatient clinic became invaluable in assisting my clients through a tangled maze of housing situations. Be it helping a family threatened with eviction or working with property managers addressing problem residents, the ability to read and properly respond to emotions makes all the difference.

My mindfulness practice played a key role during these years as well, particularly when it came to helping me become more resilient. Working with this same population of mandated clients, the prevailing attitude has been that the approach should be pragmatic and immediate, something akin to a sterile, stress management technique. This is where the Tri-Sigma Approach started to take real shape as I observed how limiting that prevailing mindset had been.

I took a cue from one of the most difficult transitions in my life: from Director of Admissions to Vice President of Operations. I was highly stressed and seem to find myself caught up in mental loops of planning and worry. I carried away a very important lesson (sometimes exclaiming to myself!): an act of meditation is better than contemplation. Just sitting around worrying about a particular issue wasn't getting me anywhere. What I needed was the practice of being present-minded.

This insight—the difference between meditation and contemplation—came with one particularly precarious situation involving an unhoused client at the outpatient clinic: he was angry and resistant, and he had missed several appointments. My mind wanted to contemplate all sorts of possible solutions, but first I observed. I actually saw his situation without racing to fix it. This simple act of mindful observation changed everything about how I approached the case.

While working up the management ranks, I grew to appreciate how a lot of executives wimp out through overthinking. "Think less, do more" became my mantra. But doing more didn't mean becoming a wild actor. It meant taking mindful action based on clear observation. The leaders that influenced me most demonstrated this balance—they were present and aware, but also decisive and action-oriented.

Building resilience through mindfulness is not about reaching some sort of perfect, calm state. I first learned this while handling CPS cases. Yes, the emotional intensity could be overwhelming. But by developing the capacity to stay present, it becomes possible to live the Tri-Sigma Approach: observe, accept, adapt.

When I opened my own private practice after all those years in executive leadership, these lessons came right along with me. Clients would often come in seeking some sort of magic bullet solution. I end up teaching them the very same mindfulness-based resilience that I learned in the trenches of the outpatient world. First, I observe their situations without judgment. Then, I work on accepting what I've observed, even if I don't like it. Finally, I focus on adapting—taking mindful action based on this seeing and acceptance.

Moving into affordable housing introduced different challenges that pushed me in other ways. After several years of service on the board of directors, taking a leadership role presented me with the opportunity to apply my mindfulness practices to various contexts; the basic principles are the same—observe, accept, adapt—yet the application differs in situation and context.

I recall one such impossible-sounding project with twisted regulations, resistant community members, and tight deadlines. Rather than getting lost in anxiety and endless planning, I applied the Tri-Sigma Approach. I took time to clearly observe all aspects of the situation; then, I accepted the reality of our challenges rather than wishing things were different. I adapted this clear understanding and

CHAPTER 4: EMOTIONAL INTELLIGENCE AND RESILIENCE

was able to move forward with confidence.

One deep realization about resilience emerged from working with resistant-to-treatment mandated clients. Most of the more traditional approaches emphasize building motivation or the overcoming of resistance. What I found was that starting with an observation—truly seeing where people are without trying to change them—builds more resilience in the clients and the staff themselves. The connection with resilience became even deeper as I began building my private practice. When the housing organization approached me to return to an executive role, I realized how my mindfulness practice supported me in considering this transition. Rather than falling into fruitless pros and cons lists or endless analysis, I saw the opportunity clearly, accepted the challenges it would present, and worked out how to adapt my plans accordingly.

Running a consulting business with property managers in affordable housing taught me how this resilience via mindfulness could be taught hands-on. When working through some very difficult residents or complex situations, I teach the managers the same principles I learned in behavioral health: observe the situation, allow the reality of what is happening to sink in, then adapt an approach based on this understanding.

I learned the most powerful lessons on resilience in the toughest situations. In the intensive outpatient clinic, my staff and I worked with patients living through the worst phases of their lives. Through these experiences, I learned that resilience is not about avoiding difficulty; it is about developing the ability to stay present and responsive to whatever comes up.

It was during those hectic days in the state-funded intensive outpatient clinic that my research on compassion satisfaction came into sharper relief. In working with mandated clients who were facing DWI charges, experiencing homelessness, or dealing with CPS hearings, a fascinating phenomenon kept reappearing among the counseling staff. A few staff members maintained their intention to serve and found satisfaction, while others showed signs of burnout in short order. This observation led me to study what makes the difference.

My research revealed a surprising finding: it wasn't lighter or less difficult caseloads that contributed to compassion satisfaction. Rather, research shows that professionals who practice the Tri-Sigma Approach—observing, accepting, and adapting—are able to stay in their posts and enjoy their work. They observe their reactions to difficult situations without judgment, accept the reality of their feelings, and adapt their approach where warranted.

One case stands out as particularly illustrative. I worked with a counselor whose clients were resistant in ways that were similar to what I experienced in the outpatient clinic. Instead of reacting with frustration to their resistance, she would note it with curiosity, accept it as normal, and adapt to that reality. She enjoyed high compassion satisfaction because she did not work in opposition to the reality. She accepted it and worked within the confines of what was presented. This also shows significant insight into the relationship between acting and satisfaction. The professionals who reported the highest level of compassion satisfaction weren't the ones who spent the most time thinking about their work—they found ways to take meaningful action. This corresponded perfectly with my belief that meditating is greater than contemplating. Thinking less as you do more often results in better outcomes.

While transitioning from the director role to vice president, I had a clear vantage point from which to watch these principles play out at the organizational level. It wasn't necessarily the departments with "easy" jobs that had the highest staff satisfaction. In fact, the highest reporting of job satisfaction came from those departments where the leaders encouraged mindful observation and adaptive response to challenges. They created an environment within which the Tri-Sigma Approach could bloom.

CHAPTER 4: EMOTIONAL INTELLIGENCE AND RESILIENCE

I'll stress that mindfulness practices were strongly related to compassion satisfaction; however, not all of these practices were formal or sophisticated meditation sessions. Mindfulness can be practiced by simple, practical methods and in the heat of intense active work. It can be as simple as closing your eyes and taking a deep breath. I reflect on the lessons from my meditation mentors: the effectiveness of mindfulness is based on how simple and stubborn the practice is, not on how elaborate your theory is.

When I opened my own practice after years in executive leadership, I tested these research findings. Teaching clients the Tri-Sigma Approach not only helped *them* but also led to compassion satisfaction for *me*. The work was still difficult, but engaging in it mindfully made all the difference.

My transition to affordable housing was a new opportunity to apply this knowledge. The challenges were different than in behavioral health, but the principles remained the same. Whether I was navigating the regulatory environment of housing or a crisis with a resident, the Tri-Sigma Approach helped me preserve compassion satisfaction in a very challenging occupation.

This study yielded an intriguing finding in the context of leadership and compassion satisfaction: leaders who cared for their own compassion satisfaction created a culture where others could engage in this process as well. I have witnessed this personally while serving on the board of directors for several organizations. Modeling mindful awareness and adaptive response positively affects the culture of the whole organization.

Among the most valuable findings to emerge from this study was the role acceptance plays in maintaining compassion satisfaction. So many professionals struggle because they resist the very challenges their work engenders. Those who could accept challenges as part of the journey maintained higher levels of satisfaction. It's not about passive resignation; rather, it's about clear-eyed acceptance that enables real

ALPHA IS THE NEW BETA

action.

Allow me to share some practical approaches to emotional growth from many years of working in hard environments. These are not just theoretical exercises, rather they come out of real situations—from working with resistant clients at the state-funded inpatient clinic to complex situations in affordable housing. Everything I will share with you has been tested in the trenches of a real-life clinical setting.

The first practical tool I'll share emerged during my time handling CPS and DWI cases. I call it the *Three-Breath Reset*. When you're facing a hard situation—whether it's a livid client or a gut-wrenching meeting—take three conscious breaths. But here's the thing: on those breaths, apply the Tri-Sigma Approach. During your first breath: *observe* what's happening without judgment. Second breath: *accept* the reality of the situation. Third breath: *reflect* on how to adjust your behavior.

I remember using this practice at one time or another in the heat of charged board meetings or tough encounters in the affordable housing sphere. Without jumping headlong into the fray, I took that three-breath reset. Within those few precious seconds, I could observe what was happening around me, allow for the leaps of view, and adjust my own communication method to meet those perspectives. This simple practice—that takes less than thirty seconds to complete—has saved me from more reactive responses in my career than I can count.

I have another practical tool that I keep in my clinical toolbox called *Emotional Weather Tracking*. Just as we check the weather forecast to prepare for the day, we can track our emotional patterns to better understand and work with them. This isn't about time-consuming journaling but rather brief, mindful check-ins throughout the day.

It's a very simple practice, but a helpful one: stop three times a day and take your own emotional weather report. Morning: What's the forecast for today's weather? Midday: How's the weather changed from the morning? Evening: What was today's pattern? This practice has helped me get through some of the most emotionally demanding

CHAPTER 4: EMOTIONAL INTELLIGENCE AND RESILIENCE

work of my professional life.

Another tool I used in the outpatient clinic is what I call *Response Mapping*. In the face of a challenging situation, take a moment to map out three possible responses: 1) the reactive response—what might you do automatically? 2) the ideal response—what would you do if you had perfect wisdom? 3) the realistic response—what can you actually do in this moment? This exercise helps bridge the gap between where we are and where we want to be.

I leaned heavily on the practice of Response Mapping when re-entering a leadership role after working on my own in private practice. Every new challenge was a time for me to notice my first response, look for the best response, then find a reasonable middle ground. This practice is at its heart the embodiment of the Tri-Sigma Approach: observe the responses, accept the limitations, and adapt the approach.

Action-Reflection Balance is one of the most valuable practices that I learned from influential leaders at that behavioral health company. Instead of getting caught in endless contemplation, I learned to set a timer for five minutes. Observe and accept for two minutes, then, with the next three minutes, identify one concrete action you can take. This practice honors the principle "think less, do more" while ensuring you take thoughtful action.

Over my years serving as a board member, I developed a unique tool useful for working in larger groups. It's a practice I call *Compassion Circles*. In making tough decisions or addressing any difficult circumstances, I envision three concentric circles representing the self, those directly involved, and the wider community. I take time to reflect how my actions interact with each of those circles. It helps me make more careful decisions, especially in the field of affordable housing, as our decisions impact a great many lives.

Related to Compassion Circles, I've also followed a simple yet powerful protocol for use when emotions run high. Take a brief pause and name the emotion you are currently experiencing in just a single word, then proceed with whatever comes next. This deceptively simple exercise creates an important pause between trigger and response and allows for more measured action.

Transitioning from corporate life into private practice and back into leadership taught me the process of what I refer to as *Boundary Check-Ins*. Three times a day, question yourself: Am I respecting and observing my boundaries? Am I accepting when others test them? How might I adapt in order to maintain healthy limits? This practice has been especially valuable in helping other people maintain sustainable professional relationships.

If you can only start implementing one of those tools in your practice today, start here with the *Tri-Sigma Reset*. Moment to moment, when I'm feeling overwhelmed or stuck, I take a minute to apply this approach in a systematic manner. First minute, observe what is happening in the body, emotions, and thoughts. Second minute, sit with what you observe without trying to change it. Third minute, identify one small way to adapt to the situation.

In a career that has grown from those first mandated clients to my current work in affordable housing, I have seen emotional growth—not from the implementation of an overly complex methodology—but from steady, simple practice. The key is to keep coming back to the basic principles of observing, accepting, and adapting.

Whether it's working with resistant clients, organizations in the midst change, or your own personal stressors, these tools help professionals balance their emotions and lead effectively even in the most trying of environments. As we close this chapter on emotional intelligence and resilience, I'd like to urge you to pick one of the practices outlined above and give it a try. Choose the one that best fits your situation at this time in your life. Remember, this is not about perfection but about developing skills that serve you.

CHAPTER 5: AUTHENTIC LEADERSHIP

My early days working at the state-funded intensive outpatient clinic reshaped my understanding of leadership. Conceiving of leadership in the challenging populations of CPS cases, DWI cases, and the unhoused means to subvert the traditional notion of what it means to be an Alpha leader. With these trying and often complex cohorts, depending on old ways of thinking where the leader is always "in charge" just won't work. This binary relationship necessitates that the client then can only ever be the Beta, or the follower. Rarely, if ever, is this the case.

I recall one resistant client situation in the outpatient clinic. Had I been looking to step into the traditional Alpha position in this power dynamic, I would have asserted dominance and demanded immediate compliance. The Beta position, perhaps, might have been to retreat and to placate. What I did was to observe the resistance of the client without judgment while doing my best to accept where they were on their journey. I then adapted my leadership style to meet their needs, while maintaining clear boundaries. This was my first attempt at the Tri-Sigma Approach, and I found it worked.

Over those six years within this behavioral health company,

ALPHA IS THE NEW BETA

the thoughtful leaders I had the good fortune to work with showed me what leadership looked like. These mentors shaped my understanding of and approach to true leadership. They showed me that great leadership is not about choosing to adopt the false binary of Alpha or Beta roles. Rather, the choice is to stay centered, aware, and open to what each situation requires.

One of the many important things I take away from my time with those leaders is the admonishment to "think less and do more." It isn't about being impulsive; it's about avoiding the paralysis that follows when we overthink. Every time we fall into the trap of having meeting after meeting to discuss all the things that might go wrong, I learned to bring us back to the present to observe what was happening in front of us. We then accept the circumstances given and change our strategy accordingly.

My new role as leader affords me the perspective of seeing how the Tri-Sigma Approach impacts organizational dynamics. Unless I pulled back and observed the team dynamics without judgment, traditional Alpha/Beta dynamics would inevitably take over, creating unnecessary conflict. Instead, I concentrated on adapting our processes to bring out the best in everyone.

My time in executive leadership reinforced that it's better to meditate than contemplate. Too often leaders get caught in endless analysis and planning sessions. I find that taking the time to mindfully observe—really seeing what's happening within the organization—leads to better decision-making than hours of strategic contemplation. It's an approach that helps me navigate complex challenges as we grow and evolve in an increasingly uncertain climate.

The shift into affordable housing brought with it new professional challenges. Having sat on the board of directors for a number of years prior to assuming an executive role provided me with a unique vantage point. I witnessed firsthand how different leadership styles affect varying organizational results. The most effective leaders were not

CHAPTER 5: AUTHENTIC LEADERSHIP

those that fit into narrowly defined Alpha and Beta categories; rather, they are the ones that can see clearly and accept reality as it is. They nimbly course-correct their approach as situations require.

I recall one particularly tough challenge working in affordable housing that illustrates this flexible observation-based problem solving. We were experiencing resistance from the community and associated regulatory bodies on an important project. An Alpha leadership style would have had me pushing harder until the Betas gave in. Instead, we used the Tri-Sigma Approach: I observed the concerns of stakeholders without judgment, accepted the situation in all of its complexity, and developed plans to answer key issues without heated debates.

I learned another valuable lesson about authentic leadership when I finally opened my private practice after all those years in executive leadership. Sometimes leading means pulling back. With my private clients this looks like standing back and resisting the urge to control the process as it unfolds, accepting the pace of change for them, and meeting them where they are.

When the housing organization asked me to return to leadership from private practice, I was excited about an opportunity to put these leadership principles in action in a new context. The traditional view might have seen this as stepping back into an Alpha role; but I now understood that leadership was more nuanced than that. It was about bringing the wisdom gained from all those experiences—from the intensive outpatient clinic to private practice—into this new challenge.

As I reflect upon my development through these discrete leadership positions, it's clear how each experience prepared me to better understand what authentic leadership truly means. Working with mandated clients in the outpatient clinic taught me that leadership is not about making sure others do one's bidding but rather about establishing conditions under which others may choose to act of their own

ALPHA IS THE NEW BETA

volition.

The influential leaders I have worked with at the behavioral health company taught me that great leadership is about breaking free from power dynamics. One leading mentor was neither stereotypically an Alpha nor a Beta. Rather than dominate others or play second fiddle, this mentor practiced what today I recognize as the Tri-Sigma Approach: keenly observing situations, accepting current realities, and adapting as necessary.

I was able to put the Tri-Sigma Approach into practice while introducing a major change in the treatment protocols that we utilized. My old leadership style might have had me forcing compliance (embodying the Alpha role) or passively allowing each department to do their own thing (embodying the Beta role). Instead, we took the time to observe how different teams operated, considered their valid concerns, and adapted the implementation plan while maintaining consistent standards. The most successful initiatives weren't driven by typical Alpha or Beta personalities; they were guided by leaders who could remain flexible and responsive while maintaining clear direction.

In this dynamic field, so many things were happening around us: regulatory pressures, staff turnover, and community concerns. Rather than revert to habitual reactive patterns, applying the "think less, do more" principle allowed us to see what was happening around us, acknowledge challenges without being overcome by them, and adjust our strategies based on the hard-won lessons we had learned.

I was still maintaining my private practice through my years as a board member. It is from here that I learned true leadership is not a manifestation of power but rather one of influence. Often, the most profound acts of leading come through quiet observation and thoughtful adaptation rather than through bold declarations or passive acceptance.

The most important thing I have learned about leadership

CHAPTER 5: AUTHENTIC LEADERSHIP

came from those early days working with resistant clients in the outpatient clinic. You cannot lean on authority or submission when someone does not want to be there; you have to find another way. This lesson has guided my approach at all levels of leadership, from clinical supervision to executive management.

Let me share with you some concrete practices that came out of this experience. As I transitioned from Director of Admissions to Vice President of Operations, I began to work out what I call the Morning Leadership Reset. Each morning before I did anything, including checking emails and attending meetings, I took a few minutes to implement the Tri-Sigma Approach. I first observed the organization as it was in current state and all associated challenges. Then, I accepted where we were without getting caught up in what should be taking place. I finally thought about how I was going to adapt my leadership style for the needs of that particular day.

This practice became especially helpful when navigating challenging situations at the behavioral health company. One troublesome instance comes to mind: we were implementing new treatment protocols and were met with significant resistance from the staff. Rather than pressuring or retreating, I started my days with this mindful reboot as a way of staying centered and responsive rather than reactive.

I was fortunate to work with one influential leader who taught me about Walking Leadership. This was a man who, instead of sitting in his office, would walk on a regular basis through the different departments—not to oversee but to observe and understand. I took on this practice in my leadership style, using these walks as opportunities to exercise the Tri-Sigma Approach in real time. These conscious walks—whether at the outpatient clinic or later in affordable housing—revealed insights that no amount of reports or meetings could offer.

"Think less, do more" had taken on a new meaning when applied to mindful leadership. Notably, I had seen at the behavioral health company how one could easily get caught up in endless planning meetings and email chains. Instead, I started this process, which I refer to as Direct Observation Sessions. This means for a continuous period of thirty minutes, I would sit in various pockets of the organization—not to critically analyze or instruct—but simply to observe and understand what takes place in each area on any given day.

I carried this habit into my role in affordable housing leadership. Rather than reading reports and attending meetings, I would often make visits to our properties, spending much-needed time observing living and working conditions. Direct observation helped me make better decisions in that I was in contact with the reality of our work—not just the papers describing it.

To this day I employ one mindful leadership practice that I developed while serving as a member of the board of directors. When making any major decisions, I use the Three-Level Check. First, notice the immediate effects of the decision. Second, allow for any unintended outcomes that may occur. Third, adjust the strategy based on this expanded knowledge. This practice helped me avoid many potential problems before they happened.

When I opened my private practice, I learned another invaluable practice of mindful leadership: the real power of focused attention. Our one-on-one work with clients requires a very different sense of presence compared with what is needed while managing a large organization. As a way to reset after each client and before the next, I developed the practice of pausing to take three mindful breaths. This easy practice proved to be invaluable when juggling multiple roles within the field of affordable housing.

Returning to organizational leadership from private practice afforded me the opportunity for integration of these varied mindfulness practices. I integrated what I refer to as Presence Pauses in our leadership team meetings. We would take brief stops to notice where we are, accept that, and adapt based on this newfound perspective.

I find the work of mindful leadership to be practical and

CHAPTER 5: AUTHENTIC LEADERSHIP

adaptable. It was while working in the outpatient clinic with the most hard-to-treat cases that I developed the Immediate Presence Practice. Whenever there was a crisis—what often presented as a resistant client or an upset staff member—I would take three conscious breaths: one to see reality clearly, one to accept the reality, and one to prepare for adaptive action.

This practice has proved invaluable as I move into higher leadership positions. Being the Director of Admissions, I faced constant pressure to meet enrollment targets and maintain our quality of care. The temptation to react with an Alpha response—always push harder, or a Beta response—be overly accommodating—was always there. But I often used the Immediate Presence Practice to stay centered and make balanced decisions.

One of my mentors took the time to teach me what I call Mindful Authority. Rather than derive my approach from a position of power, he taught me to lead through presence and awareness. When difficulties arose, he would observe without immediately forming conclusions, tolerate the complexity of the situation, and readjust his approach to meet what was needed rather than what he thought ought to happen.

Moving to the position of Vice President of Operations brought new challenges that required expanding these mindfulness practices. I developed the Leadership Circle practice: I take time at the beginning of each week to observe the organization from three perspectives: ground level, or the day-to-day operations; midlevel, observing dynamics between and within departments; and high level, reflecting on the path and direction of the organization as a whole. This helped me better understand the effects of my decisions at each level of the organization.

When I moved into the board of directors, I was astonished by how easily I could become disconnected from operational realities. To offset this tendency, I established a practice of regular reality walks. I would spend time in different parts of the organization, not to inspect or direct, but merely to comprehend and observe. These walks helped keep my leadership anchored in reality rather than theory.

One-on-one work with clients required a different kind of presence than large organization management did. I developed what I call transition moments—brief pauses between sessions—to reset attention and energy. Later, when I returned to organizational leadership in the field of affordable housing, this practice proved valuable. The housing organization had several challenges that demonstrated the need for further application of these mindful leadership practices. Where there was community resistance to the housing projects, I would then use the Stakeholder Circle practice. Here I would take time to observe the situation from each stakeholder's perspective, accept the validity of different viewpoints, and adapt our approach to address genuine concerns while maintaining our mission.

One of the most valuable practices I developed was the Weekly Reset. Every Monday morning, before opening emails or meetings, I took time to apply this Tri-Sigma Approach on behalf of the whole organization. I was able to acknowledge where we were as an organization, accept what our current challenges and limitations were, and reflect upon what to do differently in our approach for that week.

While these became my personal habits, I've also used them to shape the way I develop leaders. I have taught these to emerging leaders in both the behavioral health company and the housing organization. The key is always the same: think less, do more. I learned through transitions from the clinical to the executive role (and back again) that the practices of mindful leadership need to be consistent but flexible. While its core principles of observe, accept, and adapt remain constant, how we apply them varies with context and need.

My path to leadership has been anything but linear. I trace the formation of my professional identity to early days working at a state-funded intensive outpatient clinic and the difficult environment

CHAPTER 5: AUTHENTIC LEADERSHIP

I encountered there. What I take away from this circuitous path is that while I don't know all the answers, I know I can be present and adaptable to whatever happens along the way. The Tri-Sigma Approach has become not only a professional tool but also a life philosophy that guides and leads my decision-making at all levels.

I began to imagine how I could scale this approach in my own professional journey. It wasn't just about moving up the corporate ladder; it had more to do with deepening my understanding of what effective leadership means. The leaders with whom I had an opportunity to work at that time became instrumental in shaping my leadership style in behavioral health.

And again, the Tri-Sigma Approach proved invaluable to me. As Vice President of Operations, this meant acceptance of both our organization's strengths and limitations. And it was only in accepting where we truly were that we could chart the path to where we wanted to be. Adaptation is where the real magic happens in leadership. Once we see clearly and accept a reality, then we can adapt our approach. This may mean reshaping procedures, creating new teams, and reimagining how we deliver services.

Imagine the confounding transitions into the world of affordable housing out of executive leadership then back into private practice. After serving several years on the board of directors, I thought I was done with organizational leadership. But the company reached out asking for help, and I saw an opportunity to apply my experience in a new context.

Some of the best opportunities arise when least expected. Though my background in behavioral health might appear unrelated to affordable housing, effective leadership principles transcend sector divisions. The skills I developed while working with resistant clients in the outpatient clinic proved relevant as I learned to navigate the complex stakeholder relationships in affordable housing.

One thing is certain: leadership identity does not form overnight or by staying in one role. It is molded through millions of relational interactions, tests of wills, and choices. Each difficult case at the outpatient clinic, each organizational test in behavioral health dynamics, and every complex dynamic in affordable housing added layers to my development as a leader.

As I had the opportunity to progress through a variety of management roles, patterns began to emerge regarding how successful activities were accomplished. It wasn't because of impeccable strategy or perfect execution. Success, both my own and my team's, had to do with the ability to be flexible and responsive while keeping a clear sense of purpose. The realization of this prompted me to conceive of a more nuanced definition of leadership.

As is the same for many clinicians in my position, it is not easy to give up clinical work for an administrative position. This transition in work and identity may be hard to weather; it may feel that one is moving away from the core mission of helping people. But through effective leadership, we multiply our ability to make a positive difference. Building and maintaining systems that work will assist many more people than we could through direct service—this is effective leadership.

As Vice President of Operations, I had to make decisions that would impact thousands of clients and hundreds of staff. The responsibility was huge. The key was in keeping the same level of care and attention to detail that I had as a direct service provider—just at scale. The transition into affordable housing posed its own set of unique challenges. The technical aspects were going to be different, but the leadership principles would be the same. Success boils down to earning understanding and meeting human needs within complex systems.

What I have learned from these diverse roles is that being a leader does not mean blindly following a certain formula; rather, it's an ongoing process, building capacity to act effectively given whatever arises. And this is where the Tri-Sigma Approach pays off time and

CHAPTER 5: AUTHENTIC LEADERSHIP

time again.

It has been a progression from the intensive outpatient clinic to affordable housing. Each experience was built on the other. The skills developed in working with resistant clients helped me manage difficult stakeholders later in my career. Lessons learned regarding organizational change in behavioral health informed my approach to challenges in affordable housing.

One of the big takeaways I learned is how to continue to stay grounded in the current reality while maintaining the vision of what's possible. This is a very real tension that effective leadership balances: it's not enough to just hold big visions. We need to be able to apply them in ways that work in the real world.

The Tri-Sigma Approach helps to keep such a balance. Clearly observing, we remain in contact with reality. Accepting what is observed allows us not to waste energy fighting against what is. Adapting appropriately allows us to move toward goals in practical and achievable ways.

The approach has proved to be particularly valuable in times of crisis or rapid change. When faced with unexpected challenges, we rely on natural tendencies to manage fear or anxiety. The Tri-Sigma Approach provides a structure for thoughtful response as opposed to emotional reaction.

In my early days as Vice President of Operations, we discovered our documentation system was in such disarray that we were at risk of losing substantial funding. Fending off the impulse to panic and rush our solution, I relied on the Tri-Sigma Approach. We carefully observed the situation, collecting detailed information about what was happening rather than assuming. This showed that the problem was more specific and potentially controllable than had initially been perceived. We then came to accept the situation with no fault-finding or recriminations, which conserved our energy for solutions rather than finger-pointing. Finally, we adapted our processes, implementing new procedures that not only solved the immediate problem but improved our overall operations.

That experience sealed my belief in the pragmatic validity of the Tri-Sigma Approach: this was not just some ivory tower-bound theoretical framework, but a versatile and applicable tool that makes real-life difficulties surmountable.

Throughout my career, I've approached my role as a leader in several different ways. But what has worked best has been sticking to the Tri-Sigma Approach from challenge to challenge. It endures. Leadership is not just something we do, it's an identity. Our experiences as leaders don't just impact our staff members, they shape us. From the intensive outpatient clinic to my current role in affordable housing, each experience has brought depth and nuance to me as a human.

The key is to be open to learning but grounded in practical reality. Theory and contemplation are important in their own place, but in the final analysis, leadership is action: thoughtful, informed action based upon clear observation and acceptance of reality. Although the challenges change, there is something common across all of them. The Tri-Sigma Approach keeps proving its worth in complex situations.

I look at leadership development as a process, not an outcome. Every new challenge brings opportunities for personal growth. By sustaining the basics of observation, acceptance, and adaptation, one deepens the capacity to create a positive difference in any professional role.

My career journey has taught me that effective leadership is both simpler and more complex than most people think. Simpler, in that at its foundation, leadership comes down to basic principles of clear observation and thoughtful adaptation. However, good leadership is complex in that the application of these principles in real-life

CHAPTER 5: AUTHENTIC LEADERSHIP

situations demands judgment, experience, and continuous learning.

I am grateful for all the experiences that have shaped my leadership identity, as I find myself continuing to apply and refine these principles in my present role. From trying days in the outpatient clinic to complex executive decisions, each step of the way has added depth to my understanding of what it means to be an effective leader.

The Tri-Sigma Approach remains my core principle because it is a very practical tool with which to tackle real-world challenges. It reminds leaders that we don't have to know everything; we just need to find the appropriate approach to determining the answer.

From my experiences across different healthcare settings, building psychologically safe environments has been a cornerstone in my leadership philosophy. I saw this in my very first experiences with the state-funded intensive outpatient clinic, where the importance of psychological safety was vital to this vulnerable population. Our clients required an environment where they would feel secure despite their circumstances.

The idea of psychological safety took on a whole different meaning when transitioning into a large behavioral health company as Director of Admissions. It was here that I really started to understand how safe spaces apply not only to our clients but to our staff as well. On my six-year journey from Director of Admissions to Vice President of Operations, I got the chance to witness how psychological safety plays a major role in team performance and organizational success.

I co-led a number of workshops on psychological safety and came away with an important key finding. Psychological safety is not about being nice; it's about creating an environment where people feel comfortable taking risks and being vulnerable. This again connects back to the Tri-Sigma Approach: observe, accept, adapt. We observe without judgment, accept the person as they are, and adapt our approach appropriately. In short order, we make spaces safer for growth and development.

ALPHA IS THE NEW BETA

I remember one particularly dire situation. When I was the VP, we had a team member with a huge mistake in patient documentation. For many organizations, this would be cause for immediate disciplinary action. Instead, we took this opportunity to speak to our commitment to psychological safety. We carefully observed the situation, accepted that mistakes happen, and adapted our processes so as not to make similar mistakes in the future. This approach not only cured the current problem, but also cemented trust among members of our team, even emboldening them to confidently point out concerns that might have escalated into bigger problems.

As I transitioned from behavioral health to affordable housing, I had to meet new challenges in establishing psychologically safe environments. When I was tapped to return to leadership after my time in private practice, I found the principles of psychological safety were just as relevant in housing as they had been in healthcare: residents, like patients, need to feel secure and supported in their environment.

One practical way I have instituted psychological safety is through Open Door Leadership. In practice, this is more than just keeping the door open for conversation. It also means deliberately creating opportunities to share one's thoughts and concerns. As Director of Admissions, I made it a point periodically to walk across different departments, not with the purpose of monitoring work, but with the purpose of relationship building. I knew I needed to understand challenges at the grassroots level.

It is here that the principle of "think less, do more" applies, but with an important caveat. While action is important, the creation of psychological safety requires careful thinking over how our actions touch others. Again, I find that meditation rather than endless contemplation helps manage that balance. A clear, centered mind makes better decisions than a mind caught up in endless analysis.

As my experience working with CPS cases in the outpatient clinic shows, psychological safety is not an individual issue but rather

CHAPTER 5: AUTHENTIC LEADERSHIP

a systemic one. The safer parents feel in being honest about their difficulties, the more effective the help provided. This carried over into my executive roles as I endeavored to create system-wide psychological safety.

One of the most helpful practices that I have developed is what I call Safety Circles. That means carrying out regular meetings ensuring there are no challenges that team members are experiencing due to fear of judgment. We also apply the Tri-Sigma Approach to observe from these circles, accept the realities of situations described, and adapt our practices in order to constructively address concerns.

The core challenge in maintaining psychological safety in my leadership role was how I could continue to have personal interaction when hundreds of people were affected by my decisions. I found a path forward in staying true to the fundamental principles of observation, acceptance, and adaptation, even at scale.

In my current work in affordable housing, I have seen how psychological safety impacts not just individual well-being but also community stability: when residents feel psychologically safe, they are more likely to engage with management constructively, maintain their units, and contribute positively to the community. This, I believe, has created a mindset of safety that was imprinted in my brain by my mentors. I learned from them that good leadership is really not about making decisions, but about creating the space where good decisions can be developed—and by anyone.

Consistency is another critical piece of psychological safety. As the Vice President of Operations, I made sure the message and practice of psychological safety got consistently deployed to all departments. This was reinforced via recurring trainings, clear communication of expectations, and most importantly, modeling the behavior we expected.

One of the recurring challenges posed by this kind of leadership is balancing psychological safety with accountability. Some people seem to fear that if we make an environment psychologically safe, we are, in effect, lowering the bar on high expectations. In my experience, quite the opposite has proven true: when people feel a sense of psychological safety, they are more likely to accept feedback and be accountable for their actions.

The correlation of psychological safety and the Tri-Sigma Approach is never better demonstrated than in difficult or risky situations. In the face of a crisis, when safety in the work environment is assured, people are more vigilant, report problems candidly, take responsibility without defensiveness, and change their behavior constructively. Free of fear from punishment or ridicule for failed ideas, people are more willing to suggest new ideas and take calculated risks. This has been particularly beneficial for affordable housing, where creative solutions for complex problems are highly valued.

Building and nurturing psychologically safe work environments can take its toll on a leader. Maintaining a robust meditation practice has been key for me. It keeps me responsive rather than reactive, particularly in challenging situations. This internal psychological safety creates a foundation for extending it to others. I do it in the small, everyday choices. What happens when one makes a mistake? How do we handle disagreement? How do we treat people who bring us bad news? Each of these questions results in a choice: do we reinforce or undermine psychological safety?

Creating psychological safety happens with consistent, small actions rather than grand, sweeping initiatives. It's about how we respond in ordinary situations, how we conduct routine meetings, and how we deal with regular challenges. These daily choices with our colleagues and staff members make it possible to develop relationships grounded in trust.

It is through hindsight and reflection on my work at the intensive outpatient clinic that I was able to perceive how these early experiences framed my understanding of psychological safety. Working

CHAPTER 5: AUTHENTIC LEADERSHIP

with resistant clients taught me that safety must be demonstrated consistently before people will begin to trust it—a lesson that has proved invaluable throughout my career.

The move from clinical work to leadership helped me understand the concept of psychological safety at different levels of the organization. Successful one-on-one interactions help a person scale up thoughtfully for larger groups and systems; the principles remain the same, but the implementation must be tailored to the context. By this careful attention, we enable positive experiences and help prevent adverse ones. Psychologically safe environments allow people to bring their whole selves into the work. When people feel they can bring their authentic selves to the table, we experience more creativity, better problem-solving, and stronger communities as a whole.

ALPHA IS THE NEW BETA

CHAPTER 6: INNOVATION AND ADAPTABILITY

———◆———

I discovered the true power of creativity in the most unlikely of places: the state-funded intensive outpatient clinic where I began my career. The folks with whom I engaged quickly gave me a life lesson in the power of creativity—and gifted me with a whole new definition of the word too.

In the often stressful circumstances under which we are engaged with clients surviving homelessness, being creative isn't about concocting some sort of new idea, but finding practical solutions in difficult situations. Our clients aren't usually too excited to be there, which means you have to be creative in your approach to engagement and treatment. The Tri-Sigma Approach proved crucial in cultivating creativity within this context. At the outpatient clinic, each unique situation called for the practitioner to first patiently observe the client. Next, the practitioner had to accept the client's particular form of resistance or limitation and adapt approaches appropriately. It's important that clinicians not simply follow a rote protocol but engage in a deep level of creativity to find what works with each client.

Creativity within a professional setting means finding new ways of improving on an already pre-existing system. The six-year journey from the role of intake coordinator to vice president has shown me that innovation does not always have to imply something that is created from scratch; it can simply mean seeing things in a different way. One of our biggest challenges was perfecting the client intake process. The current model wasn't working at all, and we lost potential clients who needed our help. Instead of applying temporary band-aids to problems, we stepped back to use the principle of "think less, do more." We began testing small changes without getting caught up in endless planning without action.

Choosing to meditate rather than contemplate proved to be particularly helpful in helping to harness creativity. If we're constantly in the analysis mode, we tend to overlook the obvious. Quieting the mind results in insights that would not have emerged through conventional problem-solving approaches.

The transition into affordable housing presented its own challenges that required new creative thinking. I found many of the creative approaches that I'd developed in behavioral health could be adapted to housing challenges. It was all about flexibility and openness to new possibilities. Innovation often follows necessity in professional settings. We had few resources with high demands in the outpatient clinic. This constraint ultimately forced us to think outside the box. Some very innovative solutions came simply from asking ourselves, "What if we tried this differently?"

Early in my career, those influencing my leadership taught me that creativity is not about having good ideas, but about creating an environment where good ideas are encouraged and noticed. Many times, this meant going against the maxims of business textbooks and choosing to take calculated risks.

I use creativity in my current role by building communities in affordable housing developments in new ways. Drawing from my background in behavioral health, we implement programs that are meeting housing and wellness needs. And the Tri-Sigma Approach has played a vital role in stimulating that creativity. When we see without assump-

CHAPTER 6: INNOVATION AND ADAPTABILITY

tion, accept what is without judgment, and adjust our practices based on what we discover, we free up room for real creativity. It is not that we force it, but rather, we are eliminating the blocks that serve to prevent creative solutions.

Another major challenge we faced during my term as vice president was staff retention. Instead of instituting general retention programs, we took time to observe the pattern of why people were leaving, accepted the reality of their concerns, and adapted our approach to root causes. Creative solutions positively impacted retention and job satisfaction.

Many times, work creativity requires a balance of structure and flexibility. It's true that we need systems and procedures to function, but these should not be the barriers to innovation. The most effective way to engender creativity at work is to develop frameworks that allow space for thinking creatively. Again, it's the "think less, do more" approach. We couldn't afford to spend months of planning perfect solutions in the outpatient clinic. We needed to try new approaches and adjust based on the results. This kind of pragmatic creativity often achieved better results than perfectly planned initiatives.

My time on a board of directors gave me a different perspective on organizational creativity. From this vantage point, the various approaches to similar challenges were in clear sight. I learned that organizational creativity cannot be based on any one particularly creative individual; it can be developed more broadly and cooperatively if it's woven into an organization's culture.

Innovation does not always have to mean a massive overhaul. Often, the best creative solutions are small adjustments that create great impacts. While working in behavioral health, we often witnessed how simple changes in scheduling and communications made dramatic differences in engagement and outcomes.

The transition from clinical work to administration was a good teacher of creativity. As Director of Admissions, I made it a point to support line staff, not just leadership, in thinking creatively. Some of the most effective innovations came right from the front-line staff that were dealing directly with our clients. For example, when Covid-19 hit and we had to transition the entire business to virtual, the front-line staff was able to provide key insights to the massive shift, such as productivity- and success-tracking dashboards and new ways to bill insurance.

Meditation has made a profound difference in my approach to professional creativity. The time I give myself to quiet the mind has led me to solutions not evident when I am caught up in the rush of daily activities. The practice helps me keep perspective and openness to new possibilities, even in the midst of difficult transitions.

To my mind, creativity in affordable housing often comes down to trying to find one thing that can satisfy several needs at the same time. Programs here have been built that address both housing stability and personal development. This integrated approach would not have been possible without the willingness to think creatively about traditional housing challenges.

Thinking creatively about problem-solving often leads me to change the very framework of the question I'm asking myself. Instead of "Why can't we…?" I find myself asking, "How might we…?"

Another important lesson learned from the time in the outpatient clinic is that creativity does not need unlimited resources. To be sure, it is often these very limitations that lead to innovation. Where we cannot solve problems with money or with additional staff, ideas have to be generated that accommodate the constraints.

The Tri-Sigma Approach has been especially helpful in driving creativity by setting parameters without prescription. By clearly observing what is the case in current situations, accepting those realities without resisting them, and adapting our approaches, we begin to open up space for true innovation.

Professional creativity means more than coming up with in-

CHAPTER 6: INNOVATION AND ADAPTABILITY

genious ideas; it is all about the effective implementation of them. As Vice President of Operations, I put systems in place to generate creative solutions and subsequently test and implement them with efficiency. This pragmatic approach to innovation ensured that a good idea wouldn't remain just an idea.

The shift out of direct service into leadership roles taught me that creativity must be supported at an organizational level. It means creating systems that foster innovation while managing risk appropriately. It is about creative freedom versus practical constraint.

From my time in the intensive outpatient clinic to my current role in affordable housing, I have repeatedly watched how creativity can turn predatory situations into avenues for growth. Across it all, one key principle remains constant: we must remain open to new possibilities while being anchored in practical realities.

Implementing new ideas requires patience and persistence in professional settings. Not every creative solution may immediately work; some take time, requiring slight adjustments here or there. The ability to learn from both successes and failures has been key to the effectiveness of our innovations in the long term.

My ability to adapt to change has been a significant factor in my career success so far. My first real test of adaptability was while working at the state-funded intensive outpatient clinic. It is here that I quickly learned that no two days would be exactly the same. Each client brought different challenges that called for flexible thinking and quick adaptation.

These early and disparate experiences planted the seeds for the Tri-Sigma Approach: observe, accept, and adapt. In working with resistant clients, I learned that effective adaptation begins with keen observation. You can't properly adapt unless you understand the context in which you're adapting.

By the time I transitioned from the outpatient clinic into a large behavioral health company as the admissions director, it was a different kind of adaptation challenge. This was going to be a shift from direct client care into management, and it therefore required a complete switch in perspective. It is here that this principle of "think less, do more" came in most handy. I didn't get bogged down with analysis paralysis over the transition but forged the path ahead in tiny, conscious steps.

Mindful adaptation is not about responding to change; in fact, I learned to anticipate and prepare for it. My mentors showed me how to read organizational patterns and adapt proactively rather than reactively. At any given point in adjustment, most individuals will have moments of deep reflection or rumination. In this case, meditation creates room in the mind to observe and adapt at a reasonable pace.

The case of mindful adaptation became even clearer when I served on the board of directors. From this view, one gains a different perspective on how an organization handles change. My service on the board reinforced my beliefs in the Tri-Sigma Approach. This approach allows an organization the right amount of time to take in and observe a situation before adapting to it. These organizations tend to make their way much more successfully through change compared to those that hastily react and manage to simply get by.

In the realm of affordable housing, every day is different. The needs of the residents change, and the regulatory demands change depending on which way the political winds blow. Drawing from my background in behavioral health, the same principles apply to weathering the storms of affordable housing: observe the situation clearly, accept the reality of what needs changing, and adapt thoughtfully rather than reactively.

One of the most difficult changes we ever experienced was implementing a new electronic health records system. Instead of forcing them through a fast change, we decided to practice mindfulness with staff members. We observed how different departments were working, accepted the anxiety and resistance coming from change, and then

CHAPTER 6: INNOVATION AND ADAPTABILITY

changed our strategy of implementation according to what we learned.

Mindful adaptation requires a degree of humility. As I transitioned out of behavioral health and into affordable housing, I had to acknowledge that though my management skills may be transferable, I had much to learn about this new field. I had to embrace being 'the beginner' again. Once I could get there, I could observe without judgment, and my transition became much smoother.

Meditation has been particularly helpful in maintaining this adaptability over the course of a long career. Regular meditations help clear the mental clutter that often obstructs my ability to clearly see any situation. This clarity becomes important during the "observe" phase of the Tri-Sigma Approach. When we are able to observe clearly, acceptance and adaptation flow effortlessly.

In my years of handling CPS cases and DWI cases, one thing I learned was that adaptation cannot just be about changing superficial procedures or systems; rather, we must change our mindset regarding challenges. This insight has been valuable throughout my career, especially when faced with seemingly intractable problems.

All of these transitions from direct service to leadership required me to make many shifts in the way I communicated. What worked when seeing individual clients just didn't work when managing teams or organizations. In this case, I would have to adapt my approach. One key component of mindful adaptation is knowing when a change needs to be made and when it does not. All challenges do not require rewriting the script of existing systems. Often, little adjustments do far more than major changes. This kind of discretion flows out of attentive observation and acceptance of realities as they exist.

Mindful adaptation also involves sensitivity to the impact of change on others. In my role as Director of Admissions, I have been privy to the many organizational changes that affect staff at all levels. The observation and understanding of such impacts have taken time, and the very process itself helped to create more effective adaptation

ALPHA IS THE NEW BETA

strategies.

In the outpatient clinic, we were dealing day in and day out with client crises that called for our making adjustments on an emergency basis. Here too is the same rule: "think less, do more."

Leading a team through any change is a matter of balancing between stability and flexibility. While one may change to adapt to a situation, there are core values and principles one needs to hold onto for your team to feel confident with the change. My experience on the board of directors showed me how adaptation needs to happen at multiple levels simultaneously. Individual departments, teams, and the organization as a whole need to adapt in coordinated ways. This requires careful observation and thoughtful planning while maintaining the flexibility to adjust as needed.

The Tri-Sigma Approach offers a more concrete counterweight to what some people think is an ambiguous skill. Observe, accept, and adapt: the three steps in the process help us to navigate change more efficiently. This is not just theoretical. It's a practical approach to managing change adopted by several major industry players across various roles. I'm thinking of thought leaders like Jon Kabat-Zinn and Thich Nhat Hanh. Kabat-Zinn developed a practice called Mindfulness Based Stress Relief (MBSR) that many practitioners are implementing in their daily lives and the lives of their patients. "Mindfulness is awareness that arises through paying attention, on purpose, in the present moment, non-judgmentally."[3] We find another example in Thich Nhat Hanh, the hallowed practitioner of "engaged Buddhism" and walking meditation who said, "Drink your tea slowly and reverently, as if it is the axis on which the earth revolves."[4]

Meditation is a building block for finding mindful adjustment; it helps in developing clarity of the mind and emotional balance. During times of great change, the ability to step back and observe without reaction is of great importance. Through practice, I have been able to keep things in perspective during difficult transitions.

CHAPTER 6: INNOVATION AND ADAPTABILITY

The road from clinical work to executive leadership and affordable housing has strengthened a factor that plays an important role in professional success: adaptability. Each transition required careful observation, acceptance of new realities, and thoughtfulness in adapting to new challenges.

Throughout my career, I have seen mindful adaptation transform challenges into opportunities. The trick is in remaining aware and flexible but rooted in core principles. My commitment to professional flexibility was forged in my experience at the outpatient clinic. Here I had a natural laboratory for discovering what works and what does not in difficult cases. It wasn't academic research in the strictest sense, but rather structured observation of what was happening in the real world.

When I took on the Director of Admissions position at the large behavioral health company, it gave me the opportunity to study flexibility at the organizational level. While there, I took careful notes watching how various teams handled change. The leaders who mentored me encouraged this sort of analytical approach while emphasizing the principle of "think less, do more." Among the teams, those that practiced flexibility—making small adjustments based on immediate feedback—consistently outperformed those that tried to plan everything in advance. This further reinforces the value of meditation over endless contemplation.

It was during my tenure on the board of directors that I had a unique vantage point to study how different organizations approached flexibility. Some viewed it as a weakness and always tried to maintain rigid control. Others saw it as an excuse for chaos. The most successful groups were those who found the middle ground and flourished with *thoughtful flexibility*.

It was the transition to affordable housing that really provided new opportunities for testing these ideas about professional flexibility. The challenges are different than those faced by behavioral health organizations, but the principles remain the same. We continued to find that the teams who could observe situations clearly, accept realities without resistance, and thoughtfully pivot consistently—teams who embraced the Tri-Sigma Approach—produced better outcomes.

My research into professional flexibility hasn't been confined to formal studies. Through years of private practice and executive leadership, I've collected countless case anecdotes of how different approaches to flexibility affect outcomes. The patterns are clear: rigid adherence to plans often lead to failure, while *thoughtful flexibility* enables success.

One of the findings that shone quite vividly during my time as vice president addressed the relationship between flexibility and stress. Generally speaking, teams that committed to flexible approaches showed less stress and higher job satisfaction. It wasn't because the challenges were fewer, it was because teams were better equipped to deal with them. This principle of "think less, do more" seems to be validated time and time again. Teams that get caught in analysis paralysis generally fare worse than teams that take measured action and course correct based on results.

The limitations of a rigid approach were never clearer to me than when I worked with CPS and DWI cases early in my career. In the face of complex human issues, flexibility isn't just a nicety, it's an integral component of success.

This transition from clinical work to administrative roles afforded me many opportunities to study how flexibility operates at different organizational levels. What works for individual practitioners doesn't always scale directly to teams or organizations. However, the essential underlying principles of observation, acceptance, and adaptation are constant. Professional flexibility is not just about the ability to change, but the ability to know when and how to change. It calls for developing what I refer to as *flexible wisdom*—knowing when to adapt and when to remain stable.

CHAPTER 6: INNOVATION AND ADAPTABILITY

Moving from behavioral health into affordable housing proved that flexibility skills can be horizontally transferred. Although the challenges themselves are different, the deeper patterns of effective flexibility remain remarkably similar. Flexibility is indeed a basic professional skill and not context bound.

Perhaps most valuable among the observations of these years has been the realization that flexibility is not one skill but rather a cluster of related abilities involving observational clarity, emotional resilience, cognitive adaptability, and strategic thinking. All of these skills are developed and honed through the Tri-Sigma Approach.

As the Director of Admissions, we informally researched a number of intake approaches and their impact on client engagement. The ones that worked best were neither the strictest nor the most lax; thoughtful adaptation based upon client need was required.

Meditation has increasingly become a vital tool in the development of professional flexibility. Through regular meditation practice, one develops the mental clarity to be able to observe effectively and adapt. This is not mere theory; in almost all cases, leaders who maintain a meditation practice were found to have an improved capacity to make decisions and adapt. "Both behavioral evidence and imaging evidence show that mindfulness training can improve decision-making, both under social and non-social conditions."[5]

Meditation has indeed been an important aspect of developing my own professional flexibility. Continuous meditation develops mental clarity and emotional stability necessary for adaptation in individuals. In fact, such findings have often been consistent across varied roles and contexts. According to psychologists Johnstone and Wilson-Prangley, "Key aspects of adaptability such as learning and problem-solving suggest... mindfulness may enhance individual adaptability through Mindfulness-Based Interventions."[6]

My investigation into professional flexibility has revealed that the concept clearly means more than a departure from specific directional courses; it means stability through change. This brings me to the important paradox of flexible stability in today's fast-changing professional environment.

In my career—from the intensive outpatient clinic through my current role in affordable housing—I continue to engage in a process of observing, studying, and documenting what makes certain approaches to flexibility more successful than others. The Tri-Sigma Approach is the distillation of these observations into a workable framework. Flexibility does not imply changes every now and then. Sometimes, the most flexible response is to stay the course. This insight has proven particularly valuable in leadership roles.

The tools of innovative thinking that I have developed during my career really started to take shape while working in the intensive outpatient clinic. My work across several different client cohorts each required unique and creative solutions on a day-to-day basis. It is in these challenging situations where one learns that innovative thinking is not simply a matter of good ideas but, rather, reliable tools with which to generate solutions when you need them most.

The Tri-Sigma Approach of observe, accept, and adapt became my go-to tool for innovative thinking. While working with resistant clients, I have learned that the seeds of innovation are often planted in the act of clear-eyed observing. You can't effectively solve a problem if you don't first understand it.

When I moved into the world of behavioral health, I began to apply these more structural tools in larger systems. The mentors I had the good fortune to serve under helped me to further refine these approaches. Perhaps the most salient point learned along the way was that innovative thinking is best served by a balance of structure and flexibility, a framework that guides without constraining.

As if by magic, another valuable tool was born. In the outpatient clinic, we could not afford to get bogged down in endless planning meetings. We needed concrete tools at our fingertips that would

CHAPTER 6: INNOVATION AND ADAPTABILITY

get us immediate results. I began using *Rapid Innovation Cycles*, or short bursts of focused creative thinking followed by near instantaneous testing and refinement.

Meditation became a surprisingly powerful tool for innovative thinking. Contrasted with endless contemplation, which often leads to circular thinking, meditation helps clear the brain of its clutter to make way for new ideas to emerge. This tool proved invaluable in my transitions from behavioral health to private practice and later to affordable housing.

One of the most helpful tools I devised as a member of the board was the *Perspective Shift Exercise*. That is, we intentionally perceive any situation from the perspective of the client, staff member, manager, or community-at-large in order to expand the number of possible solutions. This proved a useful tool when we faced complex challenges in affordable housing.

We have to develop scalable tools in moves from clinical work to administrative roles. What works at the level of an individual may not translate into organizational innovation. We need tools that enable thinking across teams but that still focus on practical applications.

Question Reframing became another important tool in my innovation toolkit. Instead of, "Why isn't this working?" we learned to ask, "How might we make this work?" This simple shift often unlocked new possibilities. Using this simple reframing tool helped us to transform seemingly intractable problems into opportunities for innovation.

My early experiences working in the realm of intensive outpatient treatment with challenging populations taught me the value of what I call *Constraint Creativity*. Innovation often arises out of necessity, but especially so when resources are scarce. We learned to think of constraints not as limitations but rather creative boundaries that serve to fire up the imagination.

One of the most useful tools we devised was *Implementation Preview*. In advance of launching new ideas, teams would mentally rehearse how implementation would go, anticipating both obstacles and opportunities. This helped bridge the gap between innovative thinking on the one hand and practical action on the other.

The Tri-Sigma Approach applies a framework to these tools. The observation tools bring clarity to a challenge, acceptance tools work with reality, not in opposition to it, and adaptation tools help us implement effective change.

Regular meditation keeps the mind clear and emotions in balance. When we are in a position of equanimity, all the other tools are more effective. This is not about relaxation; it is about creating the conditions in the mind that make innovative thinking possible.

The journey from clinical work to executive leadership taught me that innovative thinking tools work across multiple levels: individual, team, and organization. We developed variations of each tool for different contexts but always maintained consistent underlying principles.

Another tool that I have developed based on this experience is called *Solution Recycling*. In simple terms, we borrow a solution that works in one environment and use it to solve a problem in another. I've had countless opportunities moving from behavioral health to affordable housing where I applied this tool.

The basic "think less, do more" principle was never more manifest than in the use of *Action Learning Tools*. We developed approaches that combine thinking and doing in brief cycles. Rather than perfecting ideas before attempting to try them out, we apply the tools in rapid iterations and then learn from the results.

As Director of Admissions, we designed tools for collaborative innovation. These tools supported teams in building on each other's ideas and focusing on workable outcomes. Their success proves that innovators can (and most often do) work well in teams.

The transition to affordable housing provided opportunities for further refinement of these tools. Working with many different

CHAPTER 6: INNOVATION AND ADAPTABILITY

stakeholders, from residents and staff to community partners, required us to support diverse perspectives in creating practical solutions. Indeed, experience has shown that the best tools of innovation are those combining structure with flexibility. When there is too much structure, creativity is hampered. When there is too little structure, the ideas developed become impracticable. Striking the right balance is key. Moving forward, these tools are in constant iteration. We must rise to the occasion of new challenges. The founding principles remain the same, while the use evolves with time.

ALPHA IS THE NEW BETA

CHAPTER 7: BUILDING TRI-SIGMA RELATIONSHIPS

Building solid relationships is difficult work in any environment, but especially fraught in the ever-changing landscape of an intensive outpatient clinic. Our clients were not usually very glad to be there, which meant we had to work extra hard to establish trust and rapport.

The Tri-Sigma Approach partly stemmed from those early experiences in the development of relationships. In the resistant client, I came to understand that successful relationships are rooted in careful observation. I have to first understand a person's point of origin if I'm going to build meaningful connections with them.

In transitioning to a behavioral health company and into my role as Director of Admissions, I found professional relationship development functions differently depending on where one operates on the organizational level. My mentors modeled consistent actions in organization-wide relationship building and maintenance.

I also found the principle of "think less, do more" to be invaluable in the building of relationships. Many professionals get caught up in overthinking relationships rather than taking active steps to nurture them. I found that small and consistent actions did more to build strong relationships than huge complex strategy or grand gestures.

Meditation became an important pillar in my relationships at work. Contrasting with infinite musings on the dynamics of relationships, meditation contributed to the clarity of mind that was necessary to be truly present with others. This practice proved invaluable during my transition from behavioral health to private practice and later to affordable housing.

Serving on a board of directors gave me a different perspective on professional relationships, while allowing me to see how various types of leadership styles impacted the dynamics of relationships throughout organizations. The most effective leaders consistently demonstrated their capacity to observe, accept, and adapt.

Moving into affordable housing brought new challenges in building relationships. This was a different context that required an adaptation of approach while maintaining the core principles that worked. What I learned in the outpatient clinic was that true relationships cannot be contrived. We committed to meeting resistant clients where they were while being available for deeper connection when they were ready.

Early in my career, the clients I worked with in the CPS system taught me how to have and maintain good professional boundaries. We had to find ways to be supportive while maintaining the appropriate professional distance from our clients and colleagues. This became increasingly important as I began taking on more managerial duties.

The transition from direct service to administration meant developing new relationship skills. As the Director of Admissions, relationships would need to be nurtured not only between individuals but also within and across whole departments and teams. That meant learning how to scale our valued approach to building relationships while maintaining authenticity.

What developed over my years in behavioral health was Relational Meditation: a practice of setting aside quiet time to reflect on

CHAPTER 7: BUILDING TRI-SIGMA RELATIONSHIPS

professional relationships in order to understand them more deeply. The practice helped me keep perspective and clarity in the most complex of relationship dynamics. I learned a foundational truth during my time working with unhoused clients. Despite their enormously difficult life circumstances, being in relationship with them taught me about the deep-seated need for human dignity. This understanding has informed my approach to professional relationships at all levels.

The Tri-Sigma Approach helps us operate inside a real framework of relationships: when we can see a relationship clearly, accept the present moment of it, and adapt our approach with consideration, we get the right conditions for proper connection and growth.

As Vice President of Operations, it is clear to me how patterns in relationships established at the top of the organization cascade into relationships throughout the system. I worked with this knowledge to intentionally create relationships, consequently engendering a more connected and effective organization.

For me, professional relationships developed quite differently within my private practice. The one-on-one situation with clients reminds me of how individual connection is integral even within larger contexts of organizations. These lessons carry on in my leadership roles within affordable housing, but I did have to make adjustments. The stakeholder groups—from the residents to staff, and community partners to board members—each require a different strategy for relationship building. These professional relationships need to have structure and flexibility at the same time. Too much structure makes the relationship stiff and unnatural, too little invites boundary issues. The right balance must be struck to sustain professional relationships.

My early experiences in the outpatient clinic taught me that the building of relationships often occurs in the small moments: a well-timed question, a moment of real listening, or a simple acknowledgement of effort can sometimes carry more weight than protracted relationship-building efforts. Additionally, as we grow professionally our ways of relating to others must also grow. What works in relationships at the direct service level may not transfer perfectly to executive levels of relationship.

Meditation has been invaluable in maintaining the clarity of mind necessary to effectively build and maintain relationships. When our minds are clear we can more effectively observe what's at play within the dynamics of our relationships, better accept those realities that exist in the present, and adapt our approach as needed.

What I have seen throughout my career, from the intensive outpatient clinic to affordable housing, is that the building blocks of any organization rest on professional relationships. The Tri-Sigma Approach provides a reliable and stable framework for building relationships in a thoughtful and effective manner.

Mindful communication practices are especially useful when working with the most challenging clients. During my time in intensive outpatient settings, I learned that it is less about what one says and more about how present one is while saying it. Our clients need a level of communication above and beyond actual words. I found that communication broke down the moment we rushed into saying something before observing and understanding the state of mind a client was presenting. Due to this observation, communication became more mindful.

These habits of communication translated and scaled when, as Director of Admissions, I moved to the behavioral health company. The leaders who mentored me showed me how mindful communication could transform the culture of an organization. Their influence on my communication style was profound. I learned about the dangers of getting lost in overthinking. Trying to anticipate what your communication partner might say instead of being present is antithetical to the Tri-Sigma Approach. Meditation is helpful in putting this approach into practice.

As a member of the board of directors, I got a front-row seat

CHAPTER 7: BUILDING TRI-SIGMA RELATIONSHIPS

experiencing different styles of communication and how these styles affected the dynamics within an organization. The most effective communicators were not necessarily those who were the most articulate but those who practiced mindful presence in their interactions.

One particularly helpful behavior that I cultivated in the outpatient setting was what I call Pause, Observe, Respond. I would stop for a moment before responding to any important message, take a close look, and then answer. Incorporating a mindful moment for reflection before responding helped me to avoid many communication errors.

Working with resistant clients taught me the importance of non-verbal communication. Often, what isn't said is just as important as what is. This awareness became even more crucial as I moved into leadership roles, where even the subtlest non-verbal cues could have significant impacts.

Moving into administration meant a change in my communication style. Transitioning into an administrative role meant that communication would now have to go from one-on-one interaction to teams and departments. The core was the same, but the application had to be different. As a team member, you mostly share updates or request help. As a leader, your role shifts to setting direction, motivating others, and shaping culture. You must communicate the "why" behind decisions, not just the "what" or "how."

The regular practice of meditation improved my mindful communication. Meditation cleared the mental clutter that might otherwise have prevented me from being fully present in a conversation. This new skill became invaluable in complex negotiations and difficult discussions.

One important skill I honed while working with the unhoused was that any attempt at communication must be built on the recognition of a shared humanity. Whoever it is sitting across from me—whether CEO or a client looking for a place to stay for the week—deserves to be recognized and respected for their inherent dignity and worth as a human being. In practice, this same principle has been guiding my modes of communication throughout my life.

A growing private practice afforded me new opportunities to hone my communication practices. Working one-on-one with clients reminded me of the power of focused, mindful communication. The Tri-Sigma Approach offers us practical insight into mindful communication. We must have the clarity of mind to observe the dynamics of communication clearly, accept the reality of communication styles being different, and modify our approach. This three-pronged approach sets the conditions for more effective dialogue.

While working as an executive in operations, I first noticed how the patterns of communication at the leadership level filter down into the organization. I implemented a more intentional act of communication, striving for mindfulness and presence in all of my dealings with colleagues.

I began developing this new approach for communication practices in the housing sector, whether I was communicating with a resident, staff member, or community partner. I also developed a practice of *Communication Centering*. Before big meetings and discussions, I center myself with brief meditations so that I am in a vigilant state during the conversation.

When applying the "think less, do more" principle in communication, you have to find the right balance between being thoughtful and being spontaneous. Too much analysis makes for stilted and artificial communication, and it prevents the speaker from being truly mindful in the moment. Sometimes, few words are needed, or none at all—a thoughtful silence can speak volumes. This understanding has shaped my communication style throughout my career. While communication must be framed differently in each context, authenticity should never be sacrificed. What works in the therapy room needs modification for the boardroom, but the core principle of mindful

CHAPTER 7: BUILDING TRI-SIGMA RELATIONSHIPS

presence remains constant. Meditation helps create the mental space needed for truly mindful communication, not just reactive exchanges. I have seen how a reflective manner of communication forms the bedrock upon which successful professional relationships are founded.

The intensive outpatient clinic was a starting point where I let authentic connections govern my work. People can sense when you are not being genuine with them. Likewise, they know when you're being honest. Even though our clients weren't excited to be there, they always recognized when someone was genuinely wanting to help their situation.

The Tri-Sigma Approach—developed from these early experiences in the building of real connections—always starts with observation. When applied to communication practices, there's no difference. I learned that honest observation plants the seeds of real connection. You need to see your clients as they are and not as you want them to be.

After moving into behavioral health, my new challenge became maintaining authenticity while working in larger groups. My mentors taught me how to scale authentic connection without losing the essence of it. What worked best in forging relationships was the principle of "think less, do more." The leaders who seemed to over-analyze a relationship or attempt to live by formulas did not fare well. This simple and genuine approach leads to better, more authentic, connections every time.

Serving on the board of directors allowed me to observe different leadership styles and their impact on the authenticity of organizational relationships. Indeed, leaders who could keep the ties with their teams real, even in a more formal setting, always produced better outcomes than others who prefer to keep everything strictly professional and remote.

In the outpatient clinic I learned that real connections require an element of vulnerability. In working with resistant clients, my ability to be vulnerable was exactly what worked to bridge the gap and show clients a reason to trust. This has continued to guide me throughout my career.

Meditation also carved the path to true connection. Unlike the thoughts that had me strategically attempting to leverage relationships, meditation helped me make room for real presence with my colleagues and clients.

More than anything, it was working with unhoused clients that taught me that authentic connection goes beyond circumstance. Perhaps surprising to some, it is this client population that I found to be the most capable of genuine relationships once respect and authenticity had been extended to them.

I carried this insight into my private practice. Working directly with clients again reminded me why I sought to work as a helping professional in the first place. The Tri-Sigma Approach provides a practical framework in building genuine relationships: where observation is clear, where people are accepted, and adaptation is thoughtfully implemented, authentic connection naturally follows.

As Vice President of Operations, I had the unique opportunity to witness how authentic connection at the leadership level permeates all levels of an organization. When leaders model what it looks and feels like to be genuinely connected, it produces a ripple that changes organizational culture. It meant building authentic connections that accommodated new contexts while retaining core principles.

One of the helpful pieces that came from that experience was what I call *Connection Anchoring*. That is, anchoring in one's whole being while moving through various professional contexts. It's about being connected but not losing professional boundaries. Real connections with people often happen in unplanned moments. Sometimes five minutes of sincerity builds more trust than hours of formalities.

One of the most important lessons learned in my time at the clinic was around workplace dynamics. In working with clients who have CPS or DWI cases, as well as clients who are unhoused, it wasn't

CHAPTER 7: BUILDING TRI-SIGMA RELATIONSHIPS

merely about the dynamics of office politics but rather how people and systems interact with one another. Though our clients' circumstances were often dire, the way our team worked together often made all the difference in the world.

The Tri-Sigma Approach of observe, accept, and adapt partially emerged from dealing with crucial and complex workplace dynamics. I learned that successful navigation of those relationships starts with seeking to understand the existing dynamics before being able to work effectively within them.

As Director of Admissions, I learned how to read an organization and manage organizational dynamics effectively. Too many professionals become paralyzed by overanalyzing the office dynamics and trying to predict how things might go wrong. Generally, I find that mindful action informed by clear observation works far more effectively than endless strategic planning.

I gained insight into organizational dynamics from my unique vantage point as a leader. I saw how other levels of the organization interacted and how these interactions influenced overall performance.

Meditation proved to be an invaluable tool in navigating workplace dynamics. In trying to ignore the constant pull to overanalyze office dynamics, meditation helped me maintain mental clarity.

Working with resistant populations taught me that the dynamics we witness within the workplace often reflect the dynamics we find in other aspects of life. Surprisingly, the skills learned from working with resistant clients readily transferred to management of complex organizational relationships. I had to learn to navigate not only the internal relationships within my team but also across departments and hierarchies. The Tri-Sigma Approach provided the framework for understanding and working with these complex relationships.

One of the more important things I have picked up early on in my career is how informal networks function within an office. Operating just below the surface of the official organizational chart, in every workplace there is invariably an unofficial channel of communication and influence—one that needs to be understood and respected. Early in the outpatient clinic, I was able to understand some of the more hidden workplace dynamics in smaller moments. If one pays attention to these subtle interactions, one gains valuable insights that lead to more effective leadership within an organization.

In my private practice, I enjoyed the advantage of having an outsider's view of workplace dynamics. I had the good fortune to have a client base who shared their experiences working in disparate kinds of organizations, affording insight into common patterns and strategies for effective ways to navigate workplace cultures.

Moving to affordable housing brought about new challenges in understanding workplace dynamics. Every sector has its own unwritten rules and its own expectations, fortunately the Tri-Sigma Approach principles operate just the same.

One's leadership style impacts workplace dynamics in every area of an organization. When leaders model effective navigation through relationship conflict, it ripples positively through a system. But understanding workplace dynamics is not just about conflict management; it involves creating the environment and conditions in which positive relationships develop and flourish. In particular, this was important in affordable housing since the quality of workplace relationships so intimately impacts resident experience.

The Tri-Sigma Approach provides the lens through which we can see workplace dynamics clearly: when one observes clearly, accepts the variety of style and personality, and alters one's approach to achieve better outcomes, favorable conditions are created.

One of the ways I was able to create favorable conditions for collaboration was through what I call *Dynamic Mapping*. It involves taking time to regularly understand how different parts of an organization interact and influence one another. This helps one to navigate complex situations more effectively. The notion of "think less, do more"

CHAPTER 7: BUILDING TRI-SIGMA RELATIONSHIPS

in workplace dynamics is not about acting without thought; rather, it is about finding balance between analysis and action. Too much analysis will paralyze, while thoughtful action often clears up situations naturally.

It is the understanding of workplace dynamics that makes or breaks the success of a leader. From serving in the intensive outpatient clinic to leading a non-profit affordable housing organization, I've been able to take the skills I developed early on and apply them to many of my subsequent positions.

ALPHA IS THE NEW BETA

CHAPTER 8: SUSTAINABLE SUCCESS

My definition of personal success has radically changed since working at the intensive outpatient clinic. Success is not always measurable by the simple act of closing out "completed" case files. Traditional metrics do not often assess what is most important. Sometimes, while working with a client, a small shift in perspective for them was more important than meeting the formal program requirements.

When I moved to the large behavioral health company, my success metrics needed similar reframing. I learned this important reframing precept from my mentors: true success requires looking beyond traditional performance indicators. Most professionals get tangled up developing fancy measurement systems instead of focusing on what really counts. Simple, meaningful metrics often work better than complex evaluation frameworks.

Meditation has helped me redefine and maintain my metrics for success. I understand what really matters instead of endless contemplation about what's important and what's not.

Working with challenging populations early in my career taught me to appreciate incremental progress. Success isn't necessarily about dramatic transformations. Often, it can be found in small and sustainable changes carried out over time. I have kept that knowledge close and let it define my own personal successes across the entire breadth of my career.

I developed still more ways of measuring success as the Director of Admissions. I needed metrics that captured not only individual achievements but also organizational achievements. The Tri-Sigma Approach provided the framework for developing these measures thoughtfully. I learned to differentiate superficial wins from more profound and longer-lasting success. Working with resistant clients in therapy allowed me to realize that moments of success often pass silently and unnoticed if we're not careful. They're usually not the ones we see displayed publicly.

Through my years in private practice, I was able to further hone my sense of personal success. Working with clients one-on-one reminded me of the same thing: success for each person is different, and it requires thoughtful reflection on how that success gets measured. In affordable housing, I faced a new set of challenges in defining success. I have found that sustaining success over the long term often requires digging deeper than traditional measures to really see what creates a lasting positive impact. At higher leadership levels, success metrics cascade and drive behaviors throughout a company. When leaders are focused on meaningful measures of success, it helps create a culture of sustainable achievement rather than short-term gains.

My regular meditation practice helped me to become more critical about meaningful success metrics. A clear mind can differentiate between meaningful metrics and more superficial ones. Additionally, the Tri-Sigma Approach governs how I develop success metrics. Where we clearly see results and accept the reality of what is and isn't working, we adjust measures appropriately to create more meaningful ways to track progress.

To help monitor whether success metrics are still serving an

CHAPTER 8: SUSTAINABLE SUCCESS

organization and its people, I developed what I call *Success Reflection*. This is a scheduled stepping back to allow for reflection on current metrics. The regular practice has helped maintain my focus on sustainable achievement rather than temporary wins.

Success doesn't mean ignoring metrics; instead, it means keeping one's eyes on simple, meaningful measures that guide action. I saw that success can come in many forms that were not always anticipated. Acknowledging accomplishments in a variety of ways served to broaden and deepen the metrics through which I measure success.

My measure of personal success must come from a deep set of core values, perhaps even in refutation of strict external standards. The choice of measurement defines not only the way we evaluate progress but the very manner in which we approach our work.

Going forward, my own definition of success continues to be refined with newfound experiences and insights. My core principles remain the same, but the measures change with different contexts and emerging challenges.

Learning to avoid burnout became extremely important in the early days at the intensive outpatient clinic. By nature, working with the challenging and complex cases we often see in these types of clinics can be draining. If we don't take care of ourselves, burnout from such high stress levels can affect staff and clients alike.

The Tri-Sigma Approach of observation, acceptance, and adaptation partly emerged from learning to recognize and avoid burnout. In the outpatient clinic, I saw that burnout emerged, almost imperceptibly. By learning to observe early warning signals, to accept our limitations as human beings, and to adapt our approach before points of crisis were reached, we were able to sustain our energy levels and continue to serve.

When I became Director of Admissions at the behavioral health company, preventing burnout was a clearly defined leadership responsibility. Again the "think less, do more" principle was key in the prevention of burnout. What I saw was that simple, consistent actions worked more effectively than elaborate, impossible-to-follow self-care plans.

Meditation became an effective tool to combat my bouts of professional burnout. Unlike constant ruminating on work problems, meditation helped me save precious mental and emotional resources. Instead, I rerouted that energy into productive performance. This practice became especially important for me during my many career moves.

Serving on a board of directors afforded me the important perspective of watching other leaders' approaches to managing organizational burnout. In general, leaders who emphasized sustainability tended to have teams with low levels of burnout and better long-term performance outcomes.

Early on in private practice, I learned quickly that burnout is closely linked to carrying the emotional weight of others. Learning appropriate professional boundaries while still genuinely caring became key to avoiding professional exhaustion.

The transition from direct service to administration called for new strategies for preventing burnout. As Director of Admissions, I needed to manage my own propensity for burnout while also monitoring whole teams. The Tri-Sigma Approach provided a framework for identifying and addressing risks related to burnout. Burnout prevention is not about reducing work; it is about maintaining the right kind of engagement. It became evident while working with resistant clients that feeling effective at work was as important as workload management.

Meditating on a regular basis improved my ability to identify early signs of burnout. For a mind deeply attuned to the present moment and slight changes in energy and engagement, noticing small problems before they grow into big problems is not difficult. A consistent meditative practice helps one sharpen those skills.

CHAPTER 8: SUSTAINABLE SUCCESS

In private practice, I work with many professionals who suffer from burnout. It's much easier to proactively prevent burnout than to attempt recovery in an already exhausted state. In administration, I learned that a leader's, approach to burnout prevention shapes and influences organizational culture. As leaders model sustainable practices and openly discuss burnout prevention, it grants permission for others to take care of themselves.

The Tri-Sigma Approach offers a practical framework for preventing burnout. I clearly observe my own energy level, accept limitation without judgment, and adapt my approach thoughtfully. I engage with what I need in order to maintain sustainable ways of working.

A behavior I've found useful is what I call *Energy Tracking*. This a practice of regular check-ins with physical, mental, and emotional energy levels that allows me to make conscious adjustments. This proactive approach has saved me and many others from reaching burnout.

Early experiences in the outpatient clinic taught me that burnout often occurs when we fail to heed even the smallest sign of strain. Being attentive to early warnings and making small adjustments has been more effective than trying to push through. What I have learned along the way—from the outpatient clinic to affordable housing—is that the prevention of burnout requires ongoing attention and adjustment. It's not about finding a mythical perfect formula, it's about maintaining awareness and adjusting accordingly.

One of the most important insights I learned about burnout prevention I gleaned from my mentors at the behavioral health company. The leaders who were able to sustain their job satisfaction in the long term were not necessarily working the least; they had learned to work sustainably. They knew how to prevent burnout, which was much less about avoiding obstacles and more about figuring how best to approach them.

"Think less, do more" became particularly relevant in the context of high-stress situations. Crises—which unfortunately occurred rather regularly in the outpatient clinic—had the ability to drain our emotional resources almost instantaneously. When we were able to focus our energy on creating plans to solve actual problems rather than focusing on swirling and anxious thoughts, we were able to avoid burnout.

Working with unhoused communities taught me another critical element to preventing burnout: celebrating the small victories. When working through what are often difficult circumstances where success seems hard to come by, learning to identify and appreciate those incremental gains can help to sustain engagement.

The Tri-Sigma Approach helped me transition to work in the affordable housing sector. Clearly observing what was occurring and accepting our reality helped me correct expectations and adjust my approach.

Meditation was key to not only preventing burnout but building resilience. Through practice, I came to know the difference between the productive tiredness that comes with meaningful engagement and that deeper exhaustion signaling impending burnout.

One of the most helpful strategies I developed was something that I have since begun to refer to as *Energy Investment Mapping*, where we continually determine which activities energize us and which drain us. It is not about trying to avoid challenging tasks but about knowing how to maintain energy in their pursuit.

While serving on the board of directors, I came to realize how organizational policies and culture can either promote or prevent burnout. When organizations create structures supportive of sustainable work practices, it makes it easier for people to maintain healthy levels of engagement.

Adopting a Tri-Sigma Approach greatly helps teams avoid collective burnout: observing team dynamics, accepting different levels of energy and work styles, and adapting approaches supported by sustainable performance puts groups in position to excel as a team without

CHAPTER 8: SUSTAINABLE SUCCESS

sacrificing individual well-being.

One of the specific tools I found most effective in preventing team burnout was the practice of regular check-ins. These weren't just about monitoring workload but about encouraging open and honest dialogue about energy levels, challenges, and needed adjustments. This practice helped staff disclose the symptoms of burnout at their earliest stage, when we could still work together to overcome it.

Prevention of burnout means more than just managing personal energy. We must create conditions for others to work in a sustainable way. It requires attention both at the individual and systemic levels. Different personality types experience and prevent burnout differently. Some need more social interaction to keep their energies up, while others need quiet time for energy replenishment. It is important to institutionalize the accommodation of these differences in regular workflow.

We used the "think less, do more" principle to approach burnout prevention at an organizational level. Instead of creating an elaborate wellness program—that may have looked great on paper but been difficult to implement—we focused on simple and practical changes that could be consistently maintained. No matter what program for burnout prevention makes the most sense in your organization, sustainability requires personal commitment and organizational supports.

In addition to burnout prevention, another key factor to sustainability is monitoring career satisfaction—both that of your own and your staff members. The Tri-Sigma Approach developed out of devoting myself to discovering what creates enduring career satisfaction. From my time in the difficult environment of that first outpatient clinic, I learned that it is not about reaching certain goals or positions; personal satisfaction was born of my ability to clearly observe our impact, to accept success and challenges alike, and to adapt our approach to maintain meaningful engagement.

ALPHA IS THE NEW BETA

Additionally, mentors at the behavioral health company showed me how sustainable career satisfaction requires continuous growth and adaptation. Again, the "think less, do more" principle proved an effective tool in monitoring and solving for long-term satisfaction. So many professionals get lost in endless planning about their career path rather than engaging fully with the work they are doing. I find that meaningful engagement in the present rather than constant future-casting ultimately produces more satisfying careers.

Meditation is a dependable ally in nurturing vocational satisfaction. Unlike endless contemplation, meditation helps one discover and hold onto what matters most in professional life. I found consistent mindfulness practice to be particularly helpful during my career transitions.

On the board of directors, I learned how different career paths could all lead to satisfaction. The most satisfied professionals were not necessarily the ones holding the biggest titles or earning the biggest checks, rather they were the ones who were able to find the most meaning and continued growth in their work.

The tough populations I encountered in the beginning of my career taught me one thing: satisfaction comes from the most unlikely places. Often, the most difficult cases presented me with the greatest opportunity for professional growth and satisfaction. I believe that it's my commitment to keeping this insight close to me that has led me this far in my career.

Career satisfaction is not an arrival point but rather a continuum. Working with resistant clients has taught me that even tough situations add to professional fulfillment long after the experience has passed. Through regular meditation I was able to recognize and appreciate sources of gratification in work. With a clear mind, it's easier to appreciate the worth of small day-to-day achievements as well as bigger career developments.

In my years of private practice, I have been able to help many

CHAPTER 8: SUSTAINABLE SUCCESS

professionals find their own paths to career satisfaction. Their individual stories reinforce the importance of aligning work with personal values rather than societal expectations to succeed at all costs.

My work in the affordable housing sector brought more challenges but also more opportunities for satisfaction. Each transition in my career required careful observation of that which is truly important, acceptance of the challenge, and adaptation to find fulfillment in new contexts.

My personal experience as Vice President of Operations taught me how leadership roles can offer unique forms of psychological satisfaction when helping others develop and succeed. When we focus on creating value for others, our own career satisfaction likely follows.

The Tri-Sigma Approach provides a practical framework for maintaining career satisfaction. When we can clearly see our professional journey and accept where we are, with limited comparison to others, adapting our approach with thoughtfulness, then conditions for satisfaction arise with more regularity.

Over the years, I adopted a practice I call *Satisfaction Reflection*, by which I periodically make time to consider not only what has been accomplished by my work, but also what has been the most satisfying. This practice helps more effectively guide future career decisions.

The "think less, do more" principle in career satisfaction is not about eschewing career planning; it's knowing how to find fulfillment in one's current work while staying open to new opportunities. Sometimes, the most satisfying career developments in a person's life come from fully engaging with present challenges rather than constantly looking for the next step.

I began to define satisfaction in new ways as executive roles took me further away from direct service clinical roles. Ultimately, direct service work looked different in executive roles. My perspective shifted to perceive my staff and colleagues as the people I served. I became meaningfully engaged with them. This is a lesson that has proved constant in my career. I have truly learned that long-term fulfillment never came from the attainment of specific career milestones. It follows from growing and evolving in the positions I have as I'm in them.

Moving forward, I am still finding new sources of satisfaction as my career evolves. This journey that has carried me from early clinical practitioner roles to current leadership roles has taught me that career satisfaction is at its core a deeply personal matter. What works for one may well not work for another. We need the Tri-Sigma Approach to keep us focused on observing and understanding our own path rather than following predetermined routes.

I have also always had the gut feeling that long-range career satisfaction stems from building something larger than myself. It's always been important to me to feel as though I'm contributing to a vaster sense of change, from working with individual outpatient clients to developing affordable housing solutions. The leaders that influenced my early career instilled in me that staying curious and open to learning can result in a long-term feeling of satisfaction. These individuals, after years in the field, still embrace each day as an opportunity for growth.

Serving on the board of directors before returning to executive leadership taught me how these different perspectives on the same work elicit different levels of satisfaction. So, finding our own unique path—listening to those gut feelings—is extremely important for long-term fulfillment. When I look back from the intensive outpatient clinic to this day, it has been one of constant building and iteration—each phase adding to the others. Even the difficult times acted like stepping stones to greater understanding and effectiveness.

CHAPTER 9: FUTURE PROFESSIONAL DEVELOPMENT

❖━━━━━━━━━━❖

The affordable housing industry has undergone major changes when it comes to career development for professionals. In the constantly changing landscape of intensive outpatient clinical work, I understand that professional growth is not just about skill acquisition but also about responding to the everchanging needs and circumstances of our most vulnerable populations.

The Tri-Sigma Approach is particularly applicable to the future of professional development. It was not until I relocated to the behavioral health company that I started to understand the direction professional development was taking. My mentors taught me that success in the future was going to involve learning and development in new ways.

The principle of "think less, do more" will be increasingly important as professional development speeds up. Where many get locked into analyzing future trends, I have found it's more effective to engage with new approaches. Meditation is one of the ways to deal with the challenge of changing professional growth. As opposed to the unhelpful mind loops about career prospects for the future, meditation helps sharpen the mental clarity necessary for meaningful change.

ALPHA IS THE NEW BETA

During my time on the board of directors, I was able to observe how different organizations approached professional development. The few that succeeded combined professional development with newer, more flexible approaches.

This observation—gleaned through the Tri-Sigma Approach—signified a major trend I spotted: flexibility. At every turn in the outpatient clinic, something required us to change our approach and adapt to the needs of the client. This skill is even more important with evolving professional roles.

This switch from direct service to administration meant learning new modes of professional development. Now, as a director of admissions, I found that technology would fundamentally alter both how we worked and how we learned. The Tri-Sigma Approach helped us navigate these changes effectively.

This early work experience with challenging populations taught me that future professional development needs to balance technical skills with human understanding. Yes, things change technologically, but how we relate to people stays constant.

The private practice years taught me that professional growth is becoming individualized and different for every single person. Anyone in affordable housing knows that cross-disciplinary skills are becoming increasingly valuable; we must be able to take learning from one field and apply it to another. These applications across sectors have never been more important than they are today.

Meditation practiced on a regular basis has helped me stay focused amid fast professional changes. A quiet mind is able to scan through, sift, and differentiate meaningful trends from passing fads and adjust accordingly.

In my nine years as a VP, I came to understand how the future would shape leadership development. It would no longer be enough to possess technical skills or to manage; leaders needed to learn how to navigate their own paths while also navigating relentless change in the

CHAPTER 9: FUTURE PROFESSIONAL DEVELOPMENT

industry's landscape. This requires you and your staff to develop and nurture your emotional intelligence. The soft skills I learned by working with resistant clients—patience, empathy, and understanding—are fast becoming more and more valuable in the eyes of hiring managers across careers.

The Tri-Sigma Approach gives us a roadmap to future professional development. When the emerging trends are clearly seen, the new realities are accepted, and adaptation in our learning approach is thoughtful, significant growth is the inevitable outcome.

My early experiences in the outpatient clinic taught me that despite changing contexts, some core aspects of professional development do not change. The character building that comes with difficult experiences is one example. The transition from clinical roles to those of leadership highlighted exactly how professional development needs to change throughout our careers. What works at one stage in a career may need to be adjusted as one progresses; however, the core tenet remains: growing.

Looking ahead, my vision is to see professional development becoming part of daily work. I see this occurring not in separate training events, but in thoughtful engagement with the real challenges we encounter every day in our professional lives. I also see professional development as a concept expanding to emphasize the community in which one works. We need to emphasize learning from and with others.

The roles of governance are evolving. Board members, now more than ever, need new skills and experiences to help organizations navigate rapid change. We need to frame professional development within a broadening perspective. Of course, the depth of experience within one's discipline or specialty has its value. But what really counts is how much one understands many disciplines and approaches. The Tri-Sigma Approach fits perfectly as a framework prescribing continuous learning and adaptation.

ALPHA IS THE NEW BETA

This was never clearer to me than when I was working with unhoused communities in the outpatient clinic. From the beginning, we were already starting to work around traditional workplace structures. Upholding rigid hierarchies was not getting the results we needed or that our clients deserved. The Tri-Sigma Approach helped us cede old adherences to hierarchies and make room for more flexible collaborative approaches. This shift compelled us to observe the outcomes of our changes with care and attention, to accept new ways of working, and adapt.

I saw how workplace dynamics could change at an organizational level. At the behavioral health company, I saw how successful organizations were shifting from an outmoded command-and-control model towards more adaptive models. An inordinate number of organizations are weighed down by analysis paralysis instead of welcoming change. More often than not, an experiment planned and executed with care can teach us more than thorough planning.

Again, incorporating an active meditation practice will help calm the waters in the midst of sea change. Instead of endless worry over organizational structures, meditation helps people maintain clarity to comprehend and work within ever-changing systems. Those groups who are the most successful promote an environment where people are encouraged to adapt naturally to new ways of working without forcing drastic changes. I observed successful leadership carefully balancing structure with flexibility—a combination of clearly defined processes assured quality care but also flexibility to handle unique situations effectively. I could see how one change in an area of the organization rippled throughout the whole group. All the while, the Tri-Sigma Approach helped staff members navigate these complex interactions.

One of the greatest insights I took from my years of working with resistant clients was that authentic relationships form the backbone of evolving workplaces. As traditional hierarchies dissolve, the

CHAPTER 9: FUTURE PROFESSIONAL DEVELOPMENT

ability to relate authentically with others emerges as an organization's life blood.

The meditation routine nurtured my ability to understand and interact with my work environment. With a clear mind, it is easier to see paths that encourage cooperation.

As a private practice professional, by listening to my clients' myriad stories of workplace dynamics, I hear how other organizations navigate the shifting sands of workplace dynamics. Each is doing it in their own way, but those that succeed share an important common core: clear communication, adaptive structures, and respect for differences.

Becoming VP taught me how one's leadership style needs to evolve with the changing landscape of the workplace. The old command center guard is giving way to one where collaboration is valued and guiding rather than dictating is key. The Tri-Sigma Approach helped me to understand and create the dynamics of the workplace. When we see interactions clearly, accept the reality of how people naturally work, and adapt our approaches thoughtfully, we create a more effective work environment.

Early experiences in the outpatient clinic taught me that dynamics at work evolve organically once unnecessary barriers are removed. Being open to natural evolution, even while providing necessary structure, works much better than forcing particular models. The key is maintaining enough structure to work effectively while allowing flexibility for natural adaptation.

As organizations continue to grow in complexity, so does the need for a greater understanding and shaping of workplace dynamics. The skills I developed working with challenging clients—developing patience, observing nuances, and adapting—are invaluable in these constantly evolving systems.

Serving on the board of directors prior to coming into executive leadership taught me how governance structures shape work life.

ALPHA IS THE NEW BETA

Effective organizations find ways to balance essential oversight with adaptive, responsive work environments.

My understanding of research directions in professional development began to take shape during my time at the outpatient clinic. Actual cases with CPS, DWI, and unhoused individuals provided me with real-world insights into what works in professional practice versus what looks good on paper. The Tri-Sigma Approach emerges more from practical research in the field than from theoretical abstracts. In the outpatient clinic, careful observation of what worked and acceptance of real-world conditions, coupled with thoughtful adaptation, proved more useful than the rigid application of protocols.

As the Director of Admissions, I was presented with even more opportunities to study professional development on a large scale. My mentors showed me how to marry practical experience with research insight. As valuable as the academic studies often are, I have found that action research—studying what happens when we try new approaches—frequently provides more useful insights.

Meditation has emerged as an interesting area for professional development research because it offers practical tools for the improvement of professional performance that one can study and measure. I realized how various organizations conducted research and development. Those successful ones amalgamated formal research with practical experimentation, using real-life results to finalize their approaches.

One important area of study I'm keenly watching develop is how professionals adapt to change. In the outpatient clinic, we were eyewitnesses to how differently individuals adapted to change and how those adaptations affected different results. These observations should inform the manner of training and development of professionals. As Director of Admissions, I was in a position to research how various training methods would affect the abilities and satisfaction of staff. The Tri-Sigma Approach gave me the premise on which to base this

CHAPTER 9: FUTURE PROFESSIONAL DEVELOPMENT

practical application of research.

Working with challenging populations at the beginning of my career underscored the principle that research must accurately capture the complexities of the real world. Simple cause-and-effect studies are often blind to the nuanced ways in which professional development happens in practice. But my time in private practice allowed for studying individual patterns of professional development. Each client's journey contributed to my understanding of how discrete approaches to growth and development work in practice.

My move into affordable housing was another example of how knowledge from one field could impact practice in another. So much of what I learned about professional development in behavioral health was translating seamlessly to housing management.

At the same time, my regular meditation practice influenced my reflections on research directions. With a clear mind I found myself noticing patterns and connections that I otherwise might have missed.

As VP of Operations, I had the unparalleled opportunity to study organizational development writ large. The insights I gleaned from observing how different departments and teams developed continue to frame the way I think about professional growth.

The Tri-Sigma Approach provides other interesting avenues for research. I'm keenly interested in looking at how professionals sustain effectiveness throughout lengthy careers. The principle "think less, do more" leads to questions about the balance of planning versus action in professional development. How much is the optimum amount of preparation? When do we lean on experience to do the teaching?

Early experiences in the outpatient clinic suggest avenues of research on how we build resilience within challenging professional environments. If we better understood why some professionals thrive in difficult conditions while others struggle, could we adopt better approaches to professional development? When excellent clinicians transition from clinical practice to leadership, how can we ensure the effective transfer of their professional skills to other contexts? Research with these questions in mind could inform the development of more effective career pathways.

In the future, I see how this research might direct us to consider more holistic approaches, combining traditional studies with real-life observation. Modern professional development is so complex that it requires much more than what we can gain from a single research perspective.

Looking to the future, professional development research must consider increasingly complex career pathways. I believe that my own professional journey from behavioral health to affordable housing is not unique. I see these transitions repeated in the paths of many of my colleagues. What remains clear from the research is that we need flexible approaches to professional development. The Tri-Sigma Approach offers a clear framework for studying how professionals can navigate increasingly complex career landscapes effectively.

The Tri-Sigma Approach not only helps one endure current difficulties but also prepares one for future professional life challenges. Being able to observe clearly without filtering, to accept without judgment, and to adapt thoughtfully becomes more important as work environments grow in complexity.

In my role in the behavioral health company, I began getting a feel for how the Tri-Sigma Approach could be scaled, observing its impact as my leadership responsibilities grew. The leaders that mentored me along this path helped me understand how this approach could shape future professional development.

The principle of "think less, do more" will become even more important in the future. With information overload at an all-time high (and here to stay for the foreseeable future), the ability to thoughtfully move from analysis to action has never been more important. I see over and over again how organizations embracing this approach posi-

CHAPTER 9: FUTURE PROFESSIONAL DEVELOPMENT

tion themselves in better stead for the future. The ability to observe, accept, and adapt systematically helps them handle change more easily than those who cling to rigid thinking patterns.

Working with challenging populations early in my career taught me that while the principles of the Tri-Sigma Approach remain steadfast, the mindset must be flexible. Indeed, the same philosophy of systematic observation, acceptance, and adaptation can be extended to situations of increasing complexity.

Moving from direct service to administration showed clearly how the Tri-Sigma Approach can be adapted to meet different types of challenges. In my role as Director of Admissions, I was able to appreciate how the same principles could be applied at different levels of an organization and across contexts.

One of the key attributes of the Tri-Sigma Approach is coping with increased uncertainty. The outpatient clinic taught us to be prepared for the unexpected every day. With growing uncertainty in the non-profit housing landscape, we need a methodology that can prepare us for anything.

Meditation works in lockstep with the Tri-Sigma Approach and will continue to grow in importance. It allows individuals to maintain mental clarity amidst increasingly complex systems.

With my private practice clients, I saw time and again how many different individuals could adapt the Tri-Sigma Approach to fit their unique needs and situations. This is going to prove to be key as professionals face increasingly multifaceted and unforeseen challenges in the future.

My application of the Tri-Sigma Approach in the affordable housing sector demonstrates how it transcends industries. While the core principles remain valuable, even as specific applications change, it suggests its continued applicability across other professional environments.

As I applied the Tri-Sigma Approach in my role as vice president, I witnessed how it could scale up in order to manage organizational complexity. I adapted the Approach, seamlessly integrating it within the context of emerging technologies. Of course, current and future applications will have to balance the principle of "think less, do more." Knowing when to act and when to reflect becomes even more crucial as technologies such as automation and AI increasingly alter the workforce.

In the future, the Tri-Sigma Approach will find an even greater degree of integration. Much as I found ways of combining it with various leadership styles and organizational approaches, I see more professionals across different fields undoubtedly finding new applications for it.

Looking ahead, I feel that the Tri-Sigma Approach is bound to be in greater demand as professional complexity increases. Its emphasis on balance in structure and flexibility has already created important value on my journey from behavioral health to affordable housing. The systematic observation, acceptance, and adaptive capabilities the approach engenders help us navigate any professional challenge we might encounter. Whether in executive leadership, corporate governance, or clinical practice, the Tri-Sigma Approach remains relevant across different professional contexts and will likely continue to evolve for new challenges.

CONCLUSION: INTEGRATION OF KEY IDEAS

From the recording studio to the VP office, across treatment rooms and board rooms, all the pieces of information I carry with me from job to job come together to form a deep well of professional understanding. The Tri-Sigma Approach draws on experiences, not theories. In the outpatient clinic, they weren't mere concepts. They were survival tools. Now they form the core of my professional philosophy to which I return every day, indispensable concepts that will change your life and the lives of the people who shape entire organizations.

ACTION STEPS FOR READERS

Start with "think less, do more." And return to it often. One should first begin to see the present situation as it is, without judgment. Observe patterns in your work, relationships, and challenges. Do not get lost in endless analysis but make small adjustments, careful to consider what you observe.

Meditation should be practiced daily. Start slow. Five minutes every day. Then build your practice. The key is to keep making time. You're not trying to achieve complete peace, rather you're creating

ALPHA IS THE NEW BETA

space in your mind where you can visualize the situation more clearly.

PRACTICE THE TRI-SIGMA APPROACH IN SMALL WAYS

- Observe: Spend time observing your work surroundings and professional interactions daily.
- Accept: Acknowledge current realities without resistance.
- Adapt: Create small, deliberate variations based on what you have observed.

Remember that my journey from the outpatient clinic to affordable housing isn't something for which I had a master plan from the very beginning. The journey has been formed one footfall at a time, through attentive observation, considered acceptance of opportunities, and thoughtful adaptation to each new change.

RESOURCES FOR FURTHER GROWTH

It is common to assume that the implementation of new tools for growth will be difficult and complex. But it doesn't have to be. From the vantage point of the director's chair, I've seen how many organizations needlessly complicate professional development. The most effective resources are often the least complicated. Try this simple list:

- Regular practice of meditation
- Thoughtful journaling of one's own observations
- Small experiments with new approaches
- Honest conversations with mentors and colleagues

Private practice taught me that often growth comes from simple, consistent practices rather than dramatic changes. Acquire the basic tools and build from there.

CONCLUSION: INTEGRATION OF KEY IDEAS

FINAL REFLECTIONS

It has been an incredible journey from the intensive outpatient clinic through various leadership roles and into affordable housing. Each phase adds depth of learning that supersedes what professional development can provide. The work hasn't always been easy, but each experience thickens the layers of my development.

This Tri-Sigma Approach grew out of intense need but developed into a valuable tool I wanted to share. I was able to use it to handle the most troubling situations, and now it has evolved into a framework that spurs growth and rich professional lives of satisfaction. Whether working with challenging clients, managing teams, or leading organizations, these principles remain steadfast.

My transition from direct service to leadership roles taught me that professional development is not so much about acquiring a fixed set of skills but rather developing a mindset that allows continuous adaptation and growth. The principles that helped me work with resistant clients were the same ones that later helped me lead organizations through complex changes. Similarly, serving on a board and then returning to executive leadership let me see how these concepts function at many levels of the organization. The core principles are the same, whether applied to individual clients or an organization's collective culture.

Finally, meditation has influenced my career profoundly. It provides mental clarity in observing a situation as it is, accepting realities without any kind of resistance, and adapting thoughtfully to new challenges. The move from behavioral health to affordable housing demonstrated how these principles apply in varying contexts. As you forge ahead in your career, remember that growth can come in many unexpected ways. Be open to it and remember that it's not always carefully charted. Allow it to evolve through keen observation, acceptance

ALPHA IS THE NEW BETA

of opportunities, and reflective adaptation to new circumstances. The future will undoubtedly bring with it its share of unexpected pitfalls but also wonderful possibilities. By cultivating an observing-accepting-adapting Approach, you will be ready for whatever comes your way.

    The Tri-Sigma Approach isn't a toolkit but a guidebook to professional life that grows and changes with you. Remember, character is built through challenges. Every challenge you face is an opportunity for growth when approached with the right mindset. Professional development is a journey rather than an endpoint. The learnings presented here are not an answer key. They are the starting point from which you can explore and continue to grow in your own professional life. It is my hope that you take them, shape them, and make them your own.

ENDNOTES

1 In accordance with confidentiality practices, all names of research participants, colleagues, and counselors are pseudonyms.

2 Find suggestions for beginning or deepening your own mindfulness practice in Appendix E

3 Jon Kabat-Zinn. Wherever You Go, There You Are: Mindfulness Meditation in Everyday Life (Hachette, 2023).

4 Thich Nhat Hanh. The Miracle of Mindfulness (Beacon Press, 1999).

5 Si Liu, Yaozhong Liu, and Yakun Ni. (2018). "A Review of Mindfulness Improves Decision Making and Future Prospects." Psychology 9, 229–248. doi:10.4236/psych.2018.92015.

6 Rhys Johnstone and Anthony Wilson-Prangley. "The relationship between mindfulness and individual adaptability in the workplace." South African Journal of Business Management 52, no. 1 (July 2021): a2421. doi: 10.4102/ sajbm.v52i1.2421

7 https://eric.ed.gov/?q=mindfulness&ff1=souProQuest+LLC&pg=4&id=ED649336

ALPHA IS THE NEW BETA

APPENDICES

APPENDIX A: RESEARCH METHODOLOGY

My doctoral research on mindfulness and professional identity as predictors of compassion satisfaction emerged from my experiences in behavioral health and executive leadership.[7] For practitioners in the field, what follows is the approach and methodology.

Research Design
I used a quantitative approach to study counselors-in-training, drawing from my experience working with new professionals at a state-funded intensive outpatient clinic. The study examined how mindfulness practices and professional identity development influenced compassion satisfaction among emerging professionals.

Data Collection
Working with 150 counselors-in-training, I used three main assessment tools:
- The Five-Facet Mindfulness Questionnaire to measure mindfulness practices

ALPHA IS THE NEW BETA

- The Professional Identity Five-Factor Scale to assess professional identity development
- The Professional Quality of Life Scale to measure compassion satisfaction

The combination of these tools allowed me to examine how mindfulness and professional identity work together to support professional well-being.

Analysis Approach

Using statistical analysis, I looked for patterns in how mindfulness practices and professional identity development predicted compassion satisfaction. This analysis confirmed the value of the Tri-Sigma Approach that I developed through practical experience.

APPENDIX B: MINDFULNESS EXERCISES

These exercises emerged from my work in both personal and professional settings. Each one can be used to support the Tri-Sigma Approach. Experiment. See which practices work for you. What's important is practicing whichever one feels right to you every day.

Three-Breath Reset

- First breath: Observe your current state and situation
- Second breath: Accept what you notice without judgment
- Third breath: Consider how to adapt your approach

Daily Presence Practice

- Morning: Observe your energy and intentions for the day
- Midday: Check in with your current state and needs
- Evening: Review and reflect on patterns and responses

Leadership Presence Exercise

At the start of each leadership task, take three minutes to mindfully consider your next steps:

- First minute: Observe the situation clearly
- Second minute: Accept current realities
- Third minute: Plan adaptive responses

APPENDIX C: PROFESSIONAL IDENTITY ASSESSMENT TOOLS

These assessment tools evolved from my work with professionals at various stages of development.

Self-Assessment

Reflect on these questions regularly:

- How do your current roles align with your values?
- Where do you feel most authentic in your work?
- What aspects of your work energize or drain you?

Professional Development

Track your growth across three dimensions:

- Technical skills and knowledge
- Relationship building and communication
- Leadership and influence

Identity Integration Check-In

Use this weekly tool to assess how well you're integrating different aspects of your professional identity:

- Clinical skills
- Leadership abilities
- Personal values

APPENDIX D: TRI-SIGMA AS AN EVOLVED STATE

Where do you fall on the spectrum from Alpha to Sigma?

ALPHA IS THE NEW BETA

Trait	Alpha	Sigma
Social Role	Leader of the pack	Lone wolf
Dominance	External, visible, commanding	Internal, quiet, self-directed
Status	Feels valued through visible achievement	Rejects hierarchy, defines own path
Validation	Seeks external affirmation	Seeks internal consistency
Influence	Relational, group-based	Subtle, magnetic, often indirect
Motivation	Control and recognition	Autonomy and mastery

Autonomy over Authority

Sigma types don't need to dominate others to feel secure. They're driven by internal goals, making them adaptable and self-reliant—often thriving outside traditional systems.

Nonconformity as Strength

While Alphas often play by the rules of the social game to win, Sigmas often rewrite the rules or ignore them entirely, carving out a unique space for themselves.

Social Optionality

Sigma personalities can navigate social groups successfully but don't rely on them. Their detachment can be seen as emotional maturity or strategic independence.

Appeal Without Aggression

In pop culture, Sigmas (think: Keanu Reeves, Oprah, Lady Gaga,

APPENDICES

James Bond, or Michelle Obama) are mysterious, competent, and charismatic without being domineering. That makes them intriguing.

Cultural Shift Toward Individualism

As society shifts away from rigid hierarchies and toward personal development, authenticity, and self-mastery, the Sigma ideal resonates more with modern values.

A Note of Caution

This isn't about replacing one label with another or putting anyone in a box. Alphas, Betas, and Sigmas, are archetypes, not scientific categories. They can be useful as a cultural shorthand to help us reflect on personal growth but should not be leaned on to reinforce superiority complexes.

ALPHA IS THE NEW BETA

ACKNOWLEDGEMENTS

This book is the result of countless conversations, lessons, and moments of inspiration shared with people who have shaped my journey. I am deeply grateful to those who stood with me, challenged me, and encouraged me to keep moving forward.

First, to my wife, Emily—your love, patience, and belief in me have been the steady foundation beneath every step of this process. To our four incredible children, thank you for reminding me daily what resilience, curiosity, and unconditional love truly look like. You are the reason I strive to be better.

To my family, mentors, and colleagues in the fields of social work, resident services, and leadership development—you have each taught me something invaluable about what it means to serve with integrity and vision. I am especially thankful to my team at Portfolio Resident Services and Inter-Faith Group, whose dedication to innovation and impact continually inspires me.

To my dear friend Robert, thank you for lending your voice to this work through your thoughtful foreword. Your insight has added both credibility and heart to these pages. To my friends and colleagues who offered feedback, encouragement, and constructive critique—your fingerprints are all over this book.

ALPHA IS THE NEW BETA

Finally, to the readers: thank you for trusting me with your time and attention. My hope is that this book equips you not only with new tools, but with a renewed sense of possibility for the leader you already are—and the one you are still becoming.

This is not the end of a journey, but the beginning of a larger conversation. For that, I am profoundly grateful.

—Cyrus Martin

ABOUT THE AUTHOR

Dr. Cyrus Martin's career intersects clinical practice, research, and executive leadership. With a Master of Social Work, Chemical Dependency Counseling license, and a PhD in Human Services, Dr. Martin has devoted his life to improving individual and community well-being. In addition to his thriving clinical private, he serves as an executive in the non-profit affordable housing industry, where they tackle the complex intersection of mental health, social services, and housing stability. Dr. Martin is also the parent of four children, a role that provides personal insight into the challenges and joys of balancing professional aspiration with family life.

As a researcher, Dr. Martin has conducted groundbreaking IRB-endorsed human-subject research on mindfulness and professional identity as predictors of compassion satisfaction. This study, published on ProQuest, considers how mindfulness and a strong sense of professional identity can foster resilience and satisfaction among human services professionals. His research offers actionable insights for addressing burnout and compassion fatigue, which are pervasive in the high-stress fields of social work, counseling, and non-profit leadership.

ALPHA IS THE NEW BETA

Through his writing, Dr. Martin aims to empower others to harness mindfulness and professional identity as tools for enhancing job satisfaction, personal growth, and organizational effectiveness.

www.ingramcontent.com/pod-product-compliance
Lightning Source LLC
Chambersburg PA
CBHW020544030426
42337CB00013B/976